ELLE DECOR
GUIDE

CHARMING HOTELS
AROUND THE WORLD

Cover: photo © Guillaume de Laubier
Style: Marie-Claire Blanckaert

Copyright © 2003 Filipacchi Publishing for the present edition

Filipacchi Publishing
1633 Broadway
New York, NY 10019

Copyright © 2003 Editions Filipacchi, Société SONODIP –
Elle Décoration, for the French edition

Translated from French by Simon Pleasance and Fronza Woods
Copyedited by Matthew J.X. Malady

ISBN: 2 85018 629 5

Color separation: Hafiba

Printed and bound in Italy by Canale

ELLE DECOR
GUIDE

CHARMING HOTELS
AROUND THE WORLD

filipacchi
publishing

The choice of establishments described in this book makes it a most unusual hotel guide. Selections were made on the basis of aesthetic beauty of interior design and the high quality of the services offered. This is not, by any means, an exhaustive listing, but within these pages you will find places to stay that live up to your most wonderful dreams.

Elle Decor has long been traveling from continent to continent to bring readers the uncommon house, along with totally new forms of refinement. We have found that on many occasions it is in charming hotels that our journalists, on their wanders, come across this art of living the details of which we so fondly describe, and illustrate in our magazine—details peculiar to every country.

By opening its pages to these new types of establishments—those that are extremely comfortable without being deluxe hotels—*Elle Decor* helped launch a new wave of hotels that are so intimate that you might almost think you are in your own home.

All these hotels are truly outstanding, and it is the remarkable personality of each that creates a unique sense of luxury for visitors.

It is a luxury that, sadly, we cannot guarantee will always be inexpensive.

But, this little book shows that to live one or more nights in the far-flung corners of the globe, in such havens of good taste and discretion, is one of the last great pleasures of the modern world.

CONTENTS

EUROPE

FRANCE
Paris p. 8
Savoie p. 28
Loire p. 34
Beaujolais p. 36
Luberon p. 37
Provence p. 38
Périgord p. 51
Landes p. 54
Charentes p. 60
Bretagne p. 61
BELGIUM
Stevoort p. 64
Bruges p. 66
NETHERLANDS
Amsterdam p. 67
Haarlem p. 70
ENGLAND
London p. 72
Lavenham p. 84

WALES
Llyswen p. 86
IRELAND
Gorey p. 88
NORWAY
Balestrand p. 89
Lom p. 90
Oslo p. 92
Fjærland p. 93
GERMANY
Berlin p. 94
SWITZERLAND
Geneva p. 95
ITALY
Florence p. 96
Rome p. 98
Gardone Riviera p. 100
Venice p. 102
PORTUGAL
Sintra p. 103
SPAIN
Seville p. 104

AFRICA

MOROCCO
Marrakesh p. 106
Essaouira p. 111
TANZANIA
Arusha p. 112
KENYA
Nairobi p. 114
SOUTH AFRICA
Benmore p. 117
ZIMBABWE
Victoria Falls p. 118
MAURITIUS
Grand Baie p. 120
Belle Mare p. 122

ASIA

SEYCHELLES
Frégate Island p. 123
Praslin Island p. 124
INDIA
Agra p. 126
Udaipur p. 128
Jaipur p. 130
BURMA
Rangoon p. 131
CAMBODIA
Siem Reap p. 132
THAILAND
Phuket p. 134
Bangkok p. 136

INDONESIA
Bali p. 137
Java p. 142
Moyo Island p. 144
Bintan Island p. 145
Lombok p. 146
MALAYSIA
Dataï p. 148
JAPAN
Kyoto p. 149
Tokyo p. 150
Shizuoka-ken p. 152

AMERICA

UNITED STATES
Jackson Hole p. 154
Saranac Lake p. 156
Lake Placid p. 158
Martha's Vineyard p. 159
New York p. 160
JAMAICA
St. Andrew p. 164
CHILE
San Pedro p. 166
COLOMBIA
Cartagena de Indias p. 167

POLYNESIA

Bora-Bora p. 168

INDEX p. 172
CREDITS p. 175

LE COSTES Paris

PARIS 239, rue Saint-Honoré, 75001. Tel: 011 33 1 42 44 50 00. Fax: 011 33 1 42 44 50 01. E-mail: www.pamfevres@yahoo.fr

A STONE'S THROW AWAY FROM THE PLACE VENDOME, CHARM AND SUMPTUOUSNESS IN THIS "HIP" LUXURY HOTEL

When Jean-Louis Costes became the owner of the former France et Choiseul, a 19th century town-house that had been vandalized in the 1960s, he set about turning it into a hotel that could live up to his dreams; a kind of Italianate luxury hotel encompassing beauty, luxury, comfort and character. He chose Philippe Starck to renovate the Café Costes. Then it was Jacques Garcia's turn to do his magic with the interior design of this luxury hotel that had been very fashionable during the reign

HELPFUL INFORMATION

- Open year round
- 25 minutes from Orly and Roissy airports
- 80 rooms: $300–$1,000
- 3 suites: $620–$2,300
- Restaurant
- Swimming pool
- Steam room
- Dogs welcome

of Napoleon III. By jostling styles—combining the classical and the extravagant—Garcia and Costes succeeded in turning the hotel into a place that has a private feel to it. The ground floor has a poetic, lyrical quality, while at the same time being quite a showpiece. Each room has its own character, but each shares one thing in common—warm colors and unbeatable comfort. This duet's exercise in sheer style is dazzling, and has restored a building that was once sinking into oblivion, to its former glory. Le Costes is still a trendy place, and makes for a very pleasant dining spot when night falls.

HÔTEL THÉRÈSE Paris

PARIS 5-7, rue Thérèse, 75001. Tel: 011 33 1 42 96 10 01. Fax: 011 33 1 42 96 15 22. E-mail: hoteltherese@wanadoo.fr

19th century paintings, black and white photos, and attractive oil paintings. Wherever you look you find a harmony of colors used in woolen fabrics, flannels made of striped canvas, absinthe-green cottons, and beige, vanilla and chocolate-brown velvets. These same colors crop up in the reception area, and in the two lounges, with their pale green walls and woodwork. Conscious of the highly cosmopolitan clientele, people in fashion and design, bankers, lawyers and museum curators—the owner, Sylvie de Lattre, has been keen to preserve a "homey" spirit. It is a successful combination showing that eclecticism can also have a soul.

HELPFUL INFORMATION

- Open year round
- 45 minutes from Roissy Airport
- 10 minutes from Saint-Lazare station
- 15 minutes from Gare de Lyon station
- 40 rooms: $125–$190
- 3 junior suites: $250
- Dogs not allowed

ONE OF THE MONUMENTS OF INTERIOR DESIGN

Rue Thérèse—formerly Rue du Hazard, due to the large number of gaming houses lining it—owes its present name to queen Maria Theresa of Spain, wife of Louis XIV. It is a quiet street just a stone's throw from the Louvre, behind the Comédie Française, and very close to the Palais Royal gardens. This rue Thérèse has also lent its name to a wonderful hotel housed in an 18th century building renovated by architect Jean-Philippe Nuel. All the rooms have been decorated in a sophisticated style—at once classical and contemporary—combining modern furniture,

LE BEL-AMI Paris

PARIS 7-11, rue Saint-Benoît, 75006. Tel: 011 33 1 42 61 53 53. Fax: 011 33 1 49 27 09 33. E-mail: contact@hotel-bel-ami.com

HELPFUL INFORMATION
- Open year round
- 20 minutes from Orly Airport
- 115 rooms: starting at $280
- Dogs welcome

THE SPIRIT OF MODERNITY AND THE ESSENCE OF PURE DESIGN

Using the finest materials, Grace Léo-Andrieux has created a youthful and contemporary feeling at the Bel-Ami, which fits in perfectly with the ambience of the St-Germain-des-Prés neighborhood. The interior design is not about sophistication, but rather something more Zen. It is all purity and harmony: sofas covered in chocolate-brown and olive green cloth, aluminum chairs and pistachio green walls. In the bedrooms, there are cream-colored walls, with solid-colored drapes, and furniture made of wenge. It was designed with business people and designers in mind, but the hotel's name is so evocative of a mythical Paris, as imagined by Maupassant, that it has become more and more of an attraction for discerning tourists.

LE SAINTE-BEUVE Paris

PARIS 9, rue Sainte-Beuve, 75006. Tel: 011 33 1 45 48 20 07. Fax: 011 33 1 45 48 67 52. E-mail: saintebeuve@wanadoo.fr

A MECCA FOR ENGLISH-STYLE COMFORT

If the Sainte-Beuve happens to be the coziest hotel around, it is because interior decorator Christian Badin has put his taste for beautiful objects and the subtle mixing of fabrics to good effect. Everywhere you look, there are exquisite fabrics that help to create warm and welcoming rooms. The "at home" feel of this hotel has a particular appeal for foreigners, out of towners, business travelers, and people in the fashion trade. For a long time, England had a virtual monopoly on small hotels of great charm. But today, happily, thanks to places like the Sainte-Beuve, France is beginning to catch up.

HELPFUL INFORMATION

- Open year round
- 30 minutes from Orly Airport
- 5 minute walk from Gare Montparnasse station
- 22 rooms: $126–$265
- 1 suite and 4 apartments: $265–$315
- Dogs welcome

L'HÔTEL Paris

PARIS 13, rue des Beaux-Arts, 75006. Tel: 011 33 1 44 41 99 00. Fax: 011 33 1 43 25 64 81. E-mail: reservation@l-hotel.com

A MAGICAL PAUSE

Located in the heart of the Saint-Germain-des-Prés, L'Hôtel is above all a place rich in history. It was constructed on the remains of queen Margot's "Pavillon d'amour"—her love nest—which was built by Nicolas Ledoux. It was originally called L'Hotel d'Allemagne, then, after the war of 1870, L'Hôtel d'Alsace, and lastly, L'Hôtel with a capital "L" and a capital "H." Room 13 was the final refuge of Oscar Wilde. After years spent in prison in England, he decided to settle in Paris, and it was at L'Hôtel that he passed away on November 9, 1900. Fortunately, this room is no longer adorned with the dreadful wallpaper about which Wilde wrote: "This wallpaper and I are involved in a duel to the death." The wallpaper may have won that duel, but Wilde got the last word, as it is in his name that the room was rechristened. Other artists who have stayed in this hotel famous for its architecture include Jean Cocteau, Marcello Mastroianni, Catherine Deneuve, Barbra

Streisand, Cioran and Borgès. Today, L'Hôtel belongs to Jean-Paul Besnard, who entrusted its renovation to the Martinet Firm and its decoration to Jacques Garcia. The latter has managed to make the most of even the tiniest of crannies, creating a circular gallery on each floor, with the bedrooms leading off it. There is an obvious attention to detail. "When you stayed at L'Hôtel, you had to buy into the dream," observes Garcia.

HELPFUL INFORMATION
- Open year round
- 20 minutes from Orly Airport
- 5 minutes from Gare Montparnasse station
- 11 rooms: $236–$344
- 9 deluxe rooms: $504–$687
- Restaurant
- Swimming pool & steam room
- Little dogs welcome

HÔTEL VERNEUIL Paris

PARIS 8, rue de Verneuil, 75007. Tel: 011 33 1 42 60 82 14. Fax: 011 33 1 42 61 40 38. E-mail: verneuil@noos.fr

THE FRIENDLINESS OF
A FAMILY HOME

The Hôtel Verneuil's elegant 17th century façade looks out upon a narrow street, opened during the reign of Henry IV, along which Parisians love to stroll on their way to the Tuileries. Some old beams and sections of wall were all that was left of the original building when Sylvie de Lattre purchased the hotel. She sought the help of interior designer Michelle Halard to return a genuine character to the place. Halard's design concept was that of a diverse private home—each bedroom different, with walls covered in toile de Jouy, stripes, 18th century engravings, sets of plant illustrations, and, here and there, a touch of modernity. Foreigners and out-of-towners are won over by the beauty of the different spaces and the hotel's friendly welcome.

HELPFUL
INFORMATION

- Open year round
- 20 minutes from Orly Airport
- 25 minutes from Roissy Airport
- 26 rooms: $115–$198
- Dogs not allowed

ASTOR SOFITEL Paris

PARIS Demeure Hôtels, 11, rue d'Astorg, 75008. Tel: 011 33 1 53 05 05 05. Fax: 011 33 1 53 05 05 30. E-mail: h2750am@accor-hotels.com

WHEN THE MODERN MIND PLAYS A CLASSICAL SCORE

By dipping back into the late 1930s for stylistic inspiration for this hotel, interior designer Frédéric Méchiche has realized one of his most successful achievements to date. Beneath a glass roof, in an oval room, diamond-shaped patterns, moldings and cabled columns are reflected in mirrors. The overall design conspires to conjure up a style that was all the rage between 1935 and 1940, including truly extravagant touches like these starfish emerging from the plaster wall lamps. The bar is very "1880," with a leopard motif carpet set off by a Greek key pattern. The bedrooms, for their part, have been hung with striped cotton in a range of pleasing hues—lilac, lavender, green and violet. The hotel is a truly place of considerable magic.

HELPFUL INFORMATION
- Open year round
- 30 minutes from Roissy Airport
- 129 rooms: $335–$720
- 5 suites: $700–$900
- Restaurant
- Gym
- Dogs welcome

LE LAVOISIER Paris

PARIS 21, rue Lavoisier, 75008. Tel: 011 33 1 53 30 06 06. Fax: 011 33 1 53 30 23 00. E-mail: info@hotellavoisier.com

QUIET ELEGANCE WITHIN EASY REACH OF THE CHAMPS-ELYSEES

After a long time spent at the helm of the renowned restaurant, La Marlotte, Michel Bouvier decided to try his hand at the hotel business. He bought Le Lavoisier, which he and architect Jean-Philippe Nuel renovated from top to bottom. The interior design is contemporary: sand-colored or yellow walls, printed curtains and wall-to-wall carpet the color of crushed raspberries. This conveniently located, elegant hotel will delight any visitor.

HELPFUL INFORMATION

- Open year round
- 20 minutes from Orly Airport
- 26 rooms: $199–$255
- 5 suites: $240–$392
- Dogs welcome

LE LANCASTER Paris

PARIS 7, rue de Berri, 75008. Tel: 011 33 1 40 76 40 76. Fax: 011 33 1 40 76 40 00. E-mail: reservations@hotel-lancaster.fr

A SHINING EXAMPLE OF FRENCH GOOD TASTE

Built in 1889, the Lancaster has always been a prime example of the art of living, French-style. With its Second Empire, Proustian luxury, this hotel was very popular in the roaring 1920s, due to its large collection of antiques. It is the hotel's outstanding collection of close to 80 paintings by Boris Pastukhov—Russian portraitist to the Court, who lived in Paris for several years—that, to this day, gives the Lancaster its edge of originality. Whether overlooking the garden, or onto the street, the rooms and suites exude a hushed and refined atmosphere. This evident and yet discreet luxury, together with a feeling of timelessness that reigns here, have seduced numerous celebrities, who when in Paris, wouldn't stay anywhere else.

HELPFUL INFORMATION

- Open year round
- 45 minutes from Roissy and Orly airports
- 49 rooms: $410–$565
- 11 suites: $790–$1,615
- Restaurant
- Sauna
- Gym
- Dogs not allowed

LE PAVILLON DE PARIS Paris

PARIS 7, rue de Parme, 75009. Tel: 011 33 1 55 31 60 00. Fax: 011 33 1 55 31 60 01. E-mail: mail@pavillondeparis.com

HIGH CHIC

This is not a large hotel. It is one of those establishments with 25 to 30 rooms that each have their own particular decor. The owner of the Pavillon de Paris, Shahé Kalaidjian, gives every room typical hotel names. Architect Joseph Karam has designed the hotel in a very contemporary style, based on diverse geometric themes and patterns. These show up in the bedrooms—on headboards and pictures—as friezes in the breakfast room, and even on the small bars of soap in the bathrooms. The bedrooms, decorated in shades of beige and blue, make this four-star hotel a sober and elegant resting place in the heart of the theater district.

HELPFUL INFORMATION
- Open year round
- 20 minutes from Roissy Airport
- 5 minutes from Saint-Lazare station
- 3 minutes from Gare du Nord station
- 10 minutes from Gare de Lyon station
- 30 rooms: $195–$245 (low season), $230–$285 (high season)
- Dogs welcome

LE BALTIMORE SOFITEL Paris

PARIS Demeure Hôtels, 88 *bis*, avenue Kléber, 75116. Tel: 011 33 1 44 34 54 54. Fax: 011 33 1 44 34 54 44. E-mail: reservation@hotelbaltimore.com

WHEN BRITISH CHARM MAKES ITSELF AT HOME IN PARIS

In 1920, this residential building was turned into a hotel and named after its first and most loyal customer, Lord Baltimore. Standing close to the Champs-Elysées, between the Arc de Triomphe and the Trocadéro, its elegant and masculine decoration by Christine Gerondeau lets its British inspiration and New World modernity shine through: furniture with clean lines and straight forms softened by woolen fabric and Prince of Wales check flannel. In the rooms, there are five dominant color combinations: gray and red, marron glacé and mauve, gray-blue and brown, ivory and taupe, and lastly, camel. The restaurant maintains the comfy atmosphere of an old English pub with its pale woodwork.

HELPFUL INFORMATION
- Open year round
- 45 minutes from Roissy and Orly airports
- 20 minutes from Saint-Lazare and Gare Montparnasse train stations
- 104 rooms: $340–$550 (low season), $425–$690 (high season)
- 1 suite: $750 (low season), $930 (high season)
- Gastronomical restaurant
- Dogs welcome

LE PERGOLÈSE Paris

PARIS 3, rue Pergolèse, 75116. Tel: 011 33 1 53 64 04 04. Fax: 011 33 1 53 64 04 40. E-mail: hotel@pergolese.com

A HOTEL OF GREAT CHARM NEAR THE BOIS DE BOULOGNE

Edith Vidalenc bought the Pergolèse hotel in 1990 and knew just the person for the renovation task ahead—Rena Dumas. She gave the hotel a contemporary architectural look while at the same time creating a sweet and gentle atmosphere by means of furnishings with soft curves, warm, inviting materials and primary colors. The hotel's 40 rooms all have the same furniture, and yet each is unique because of the different color scheme for the carpet, curtains and chairs in each room. To create a feeling of space, consistency in the various elements had to prevail. Rena and Edith succeeded in creating a hotel where a touch of refinement and sophistication has been added to every last detail.

HELPFUL INFORMATION

- Open year round
- 20 minutes from Roissy Airport
- 40 rooms: $200–$350
- Dogs welcome

LE SQUARE Paris

Paris 3, rue de Boulainvilliers, 75016. Tel: 011 33 1 44 14 91 90. Fax: 011 33 1 44 14 91 99. E-mail: hotel.square@wanadoo.fr

FUTURISTIC AND TIMELESS, THE HOTEL OF TOMORROW IS HERE

In the 16th arrondissement, this elegant vessel, made of green granite, gives the impression it is heading for the nearby Seine River. Designed by architect François-Xavier Evellin, it is structured around a 35 foot high half-cylinder, with the hotel starting at the first basement. Each level is laid out vertically, and the hotel is topped by a glass roof. Here, luxury is measured in square feet. The palette for the interior design, as conceived by Coralie Halard, is a harmonious blend of three colors, all in the range of brick-red and gray. Do not be fooled by the futuristic look of the hotel, at its heart is old-fashioned warmth and friendliness, qualities that modern architecture cannot afford to leave in the past.

HELPFUL INFORMATION

- Open year round
- 20 minutes from Orly Airport
- 22 rooms: $245–$315
- 6 suites: $390–$480
- Restaurant
- Dogs not allowed

23

HÔTEL CHAMPS-ÉLYSÉES Paris

PARIS Radisson SAS, 78, avenue Marceau, 75008. Tel: 011 33 1 53 23 43 43. Fax: 011 33 1 53 23 43 44. E-mail: sales.paris@radissonsas.com

SOPHISTICATION AND SOBRIETY, PARIS-STYLE

We well remember the famous Vuitton store on Avenue Marceau; it is here that the Radisson chain has decided to open its first Paris hotel, just around the corner from the Arc de Triomphe and the Champs-Elysées. In this superb Haussman building, the Ecart Agency has achieved a timeless interior architecture, at once comfortable and elegant thanks to those fine, natural materials, wood and glass. The 46 bedrooms are done up in tobacco and honey shades, accentuated by the white hue of the comforters. These same warm colors are replicated in the ash furniture, the curtain fabrics and the armchairs throughout the hotel. Noteworthy, too, is the "La Place" restaurant, which opens onto a delightfully shady garden and terrace where, on fine days, one can enjoy a meal. Jean-André Charrial (the chef at L'Oustau de Baumanière) is the culinary consultant: he has created a short menu which changes every week, and promotes Provençal specialties. It is a pleasantly laid back place, with southerly overtones in a famous Right Bank neighborhood.

HELPFUL INFORMATION
- Open year round
- 25 minutes from Orly Airport
- 30 minutes form Roissy Airport
- 15 minutes from Gare du Nord and Gare Montparnasse stations
- 20 minutes from Gare de l'Est and Gare de Lyon stations
- 45 rooms: $349–$415
- 1 suite: $690
- Restaurant
- Dogs not allowed

LE DOKHAN'S Paris

Paris 117, rue Lauriston, 75116. Tel: 011 33 1 55 33 16 55. Fax: 011 33 1 55 33 16 56. E-mail: hotel.trocadero.dokhans@wanadoo.fr

A LUXURIOUS AND QUIET HOTEL IN THE HEART OF THE 16TH ARRONDISSEMENT

Not far from the Trocadéro, secluded behind a beautiful 19th century façade of dressed stone, is Dokhan's, an elegant hotel. The exterior, with its ivy and box trees trimmed into perfect ball shapes, sets the tone for the whole. The circular entrance hall has been done in the style of a neo-classical winter garden, with its checkerboard floor, against which the box trees stand out. Emerald-green, silk blinds are the perfect finishing touch to this nostalgic evocation. The hotel's large lounge, with its bracketed cornices, fluted columns, mahogany doors crowned with sculpted vases, and Georgian fireplace, is very much in the style of late 18th century English architecture. Superb antiques make this an altogether eye-catching room. The harmony inherent in the mix of comfortable furniture and rooms decorated with the most subtle

HELPFUL INFORMATION

- Open year round
- 50 minutes from Orly Airport
- 70 minutes from Roissy Airport
- 41 rooms
Prestige: $400–$518
Luxury: $442–$595
- 4 suites:
$808–$1,067
- Dogs welcome

materials and fabrics only add to the overall attractiveness. An atmosphere of pure refinement blows gently through these rooms. Never before has the adjective "private" been quite so aptly used to describe a hotel.

LE LODGE PARK Savoie

MEGÈVE 100, rue d'Arly, 74120. Tel: 011 33 + 50 93 05 03. Fax: 011 33 + 50 93 09 52. E-mail: contact@lodgepark.com

THE TRAPPER'S SPIRIT
TRANSLATED INTO LUXURY

In the center of Megève is an island of greenery known as Lodge Park. This building, which has undergone a complete renovation, has been decorated in a most unexpected way, to say the least. Like a colorful travel notebook, the place is dotted with hunting trophies, airplane propellers, carved bears, and old-style skis. A cozy note is struck by the wood logs, stone fireplaces, well-worn leather, slate bathrooms and walls covered in plaids. Visitors get the feeling that they are staying at a lodge in the Adirondacks during the time of the gold rush. Whether it's taking advantage of the fitness center, or going for something more sporting, everything has been conceived to guarantee the guest a pleasurable stay.

HELPFUL INFORMATION

- Open from 6/15 to 9/15, and from 12/10 to 4/10
- 20 minutes from Sallanches train station
- 60 minutes from Geneva Airport
- 38 rooms: $434

- 12 suites: starting at $785
- Restaurant
- Fitness center
- Swimming pool
- 2 steam rooms
- Dogs welcome (for additional charge)

HÔTEL MONT-BLANC Savoie

MEGÈVE 29, rue Ambroise-Martin, 74120. Tel: 011 33 4 50 21 20 02. Fax: 011 33 4 50 21 45 28. E-mail: contact@hotelmontblanc.com

THE HEIGHT OF COMFORT
ON THE MOUNTAIN TOPS

Like many a great beauty, the mythical Mont-Blanc hotel has recently received a facelift. English, Austrian and Savoyard design trends come together felicitously in the singular and delightful ambience Jocelyne and Jean-Louis Sibuet have created. It is the play of light-colored wood, and thick, shimmering fabrics that prevails in the overall design to give the place its warm and welcoming allure. English furniture and mountain dressers rub shoulders while old paintings and portraits keep a silent watch. Megève's magic lives on with the return of a hotel that is on familiar terms with the mountaintops, and one that is more sumptuous and elegant than ever.

HELPFUL INFORMATION

- Open from 6/10 to 4/31
- 20 minutes from Sallanches train station
- 60 minutes from Geneva Airport
- 29 rooms: $152–$328
- 11 suites: $370–$550
- Outdoor swimming pool (high season)
- Sauna
- Jacuzzi
- Massage room
- Dogs welcome (for additional charge)

LES FERMES DE MARIE Savoie

MEGÈVE Chemin de Riante-Colline, 74120. Tel: 011 33 + 50 93 03 10. Fax: 011 33 + 50 93 09 84. E-mail: contact@fermesdemarie.com

A HAMLET OF CHALETS MINUTES FROM THE HEART OF MEGÈVE

Several chalets make up the Fermes de Marie complex, and each is decorated with traditional Savoyard furniture picked up in antique stores. The red and green fabric of the curtains and cushions brings out the warm colors in the wood. This spacious complex features any number of ways to relax—including a beauty center, jacuzzi and swimming pool. The rustic look of the buildings, the sophistication that has gone into the details and the special attention paid to comfort, lend this place an appeal and distinctive style for which this region is known.

HELPFUL INFORMATION
- Open from 12/15 to 4/15 and from 6/15 to 9/15
- 20 minutes from Sallanches train station
- 60 minutes from Geneva Airport
- 71 rooms and suites: $120–$450
- 3 restaurants (half-board)
- Swimming pool
- Sauna
- Jacuzzi
- Fitness center
- Beauty center
- Dogs welcome (for additional charge)

LE CHALET Savoie

MÉRIBEL Le Belvédère, 73550. Tel: 011 33 + 79 23 28 23. Fax: 011 33 + 79 23 28 18.

SAVOYARD TRADITION IN AN INTIMATE SURROUNDING

To create a genuine Savoyard chalet, Dominique and Michel Bisac had a building constructed exclusively of fir, with the

HELPFUL INFORMATION

- Open from 12/19 to 4/24
- 15 minutes from Moutiers train station
- 35 rooms: $104 (low season), $191 (high season)
- 6 suites: $130 (low season), $240 (high season)
- Restaurant (full-board)
- Swimming pool
- Sauna
- Steam room
- Dogs not allowed

foundations made of stone and the sloped roof laid with slate from Aosta. A wonderfully intimate atmosphere is created thanks to lots of nooks and crannies tucked away on different levels. Guest convenience was of great concern in the design, and this is evident in the elevator at the center of the large hallways. At the hub of the hotel is the entrance hall, which opens out onto both the dining room and the lounge. Splashes of red and green help to illustrate the softness of the natural wood, and fabrics in warm tones brighten the rooms. The paneled rooms are spacious and comfortable. Each has its own balcony and the feeling of a guest room in a private home rather than a hotel.

LES TROISGROS Loire

ROANNE Place Jean-Troisgros, 42300. Tel: 011 33 4 77 71 66 97. Fax: 011 33 4 77 70 39 77. E-mail: info@troisgrois.fr

TROISGROS UPDATES ITS INTERIOR DECOR AND MENU

Not ones to rest on their laurels after 30 years with a Michelin 3-star ranking, the Troisgros family wanted to keep on doing what they've been doing so successfully, but with a change for the better. With the help of interior decorator Christian Liaigre and François Champsaur—who redesigned the bar and living room/library, bedrooms, bathrooms—they reached their goal. A contemporary, and yet classical spareness hallmarks the decor: clean lines and a mastery of geometry in the furniture designed by Champsaur. This subtle, refined style is in keeping with the spirit and culinary tradition of the Troisgros, where meticulousness, inventiveness and delicacy are always on the menu.

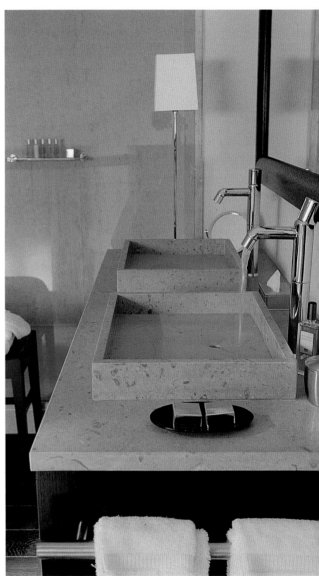

LE CHÂTEAU DE BAGNOLS   Beaujolais

BAGNOLS-EN-BEAUJOLAIS, 69620 Tel: 011 33 4 74 71 40 00. Fax: 011 33 4 74 71 40 49. E-mail: info@bagnols.com

HELPFUL INFORMATION
- Open from 3/31 to 1/2
- 45 minutes from Lyon-Satolas Airport
- 30 minutes from Lyon-Perrache train station
- 12 rooms: $400–$550
- 8 suites: $600–$850
- Restaurant
- Swimming pool
- Dogs welcome (with additional charge)

ROOMS IN A CASTLE BUILT IN THE 13TH CENTURY

In the Beaujolais countryside, where wooded dales and vineyards put on a continual and outstanding show, the Bagnols castle holds a front row seat. Its medieval origins can readily be seen in its architecture, and this glorious past has been taken into account for the design of the interiors.

For example, in the rooms that have been fixed up under the magnificent timberwork of the outbuildings, canopy beds mingle with antique objects, Provençal colonnades and topstitched fabrics. In good weather, you can sample the chef's refined cooking on the south-facing terrace, or, if you prefer, in the soothing shade of the plane trees.

LA BASTIDE DE CAPELONGUE Luberon

BONNIEUX 84480. Tel: 011 33 + 90 75 89 78. Fax: 011 33 + 90 75 93 03. E-mail: bastide@francemarket.com

PROVENCAL STYLE AND FINE COOKING IN THE HEART OF THE LUBERON

This delightful hotel—from which you get a superb view of the village of Bonnieux—holds a lovely surprise in its architecture. As in a village, the different parts of the buildings are all gathered snugly around a little square. Inside, the decor is classic Provençal: beams, warm woodwork, amaranthine walls, soft hues and pale yellows, all of which fits in well with the coziness of the spaces. Each room is bedecked in furniture featuring light, graceful lines and expertly crafted, topstitched fabrics. The carefully prepared food, made with produce from the garden, adds the final touch. Why go to the expense of buying a place in the Luberon, when you can come here, to this delightful hotel, and enjoy the beautiful countryside that surrounds it, without a care?

HELPFUL INFORMATION

- Open from 3/15 to 11/15
- 45 minutes from Avignon Airport
- 14 rooms: $152–$259
- 3 suites: $213 (low season), $305 (high season)
- Restaurant (half-board)
- Swimming pool
- Dogs welcome

LA VILLA GALLICI Provence

AIX-EN-PROVENCE Avenue de la Violette, 13100. Tel: 011 33 4 42 23 29 23. Fax: 011 33 4 42 96 30 45. E-mail: gallici@relaischateaux.fr

A PROVENCAL FARMHOUSE WITH A FRIENDLY WELCOME

The Villa Gallici lies in the hills near Aix-en-Provence, dozing and waking in the shade of plane trees. The charm of this recently converted hotel begins with its avenue of oleanders, which takes you right up to the orangery, ochre walls and gray shutters. It is hard to imagine a more seductive setting. The Villa Gallici is designed like a guesthouse. Its few rooms are spacious and comfortable, and almost all of them have either a terrace or a small, private garden. Gil Dez had a great time mixing toile de Jouy and stripes, and floral prints with checks, to create interiors that are warm and homey. Unlike many hotels where the decor can be quite impersonal, not to mention soulless, the rooms here are lively and look as if they are actually lived in. There is a great originality at play in these rooms— floral prints, checkered

cotton, four-poster beds, and slightly patinated Provençal furniture, and padded armchairs that really are as comfortable as they look. Everything possible has been done to make guests feel at home, or as though they are staying with a friend. Little wonder that so many tasteful, discerning people are drawn to this beautiful villa where, in the summer, it is not unusual to cross paths with performers from the renowned Aix Opera Festival.

HELPFUL INFORMATION

- Open year round
- 30 minutes from Marseille Airport
- 15 minutes from Aix-en-Provence train station
- 22 rooms: $245–$500
- 4 suites: $540
- Restaurant (half-board and full-board)
- Swimming pool
- Dogs welcome (with additional charge)

L'OUSTAU DE BAUMANIÈRE Provence

Les Baux-de-Provence 13520. Tel: 011 33 + 90 54 33 07. Fax: 011 33 + 90 54 40 46. E-mail: office@oustaudebaumanière.com

A STUNNING PLACE IN THE MIDST OF NATURE

You enter this 18th century manor through a courtyard surrounding a pond where stone cherubs gaze at one another. When Jean-André Charial became the owner of L'Oustau de Baumanière, he entrusted its redesign to Brune and Alexandre Lafourcade. Today, it offers fifteen rooms, each with its own style, and all furnished and decorated by Geneviève Charial and Michèle Halard. Furniture bargain-hunted in L'Isle-sur-La-Sorgue is mixed with pieces designed by the Halard themselves. Most of the ground floor rooms have terraces looking onto the garden, which has been renovated by André Gayraud, landscape gardener of the great castles around Bordeaux. He has filled the

garden here with white roses—"Snow Fairy," "Anita Pereire" and "Anapurna"—which mingle with box and olive. He has also restored the small channel that leads to the washhouse. If you really want to experience an unforgettable environment, there is simply no better place to stay—not least because you will also sample the outstanding cooking of one of France's greatest chefs.

HELPFUL INFORMATION
- Open from 3/1 to 1/1 (closed on Wednesday and Thursday mornings from 11/1 to 3/1)
- 15 rooms: $230–$250
- 12 suites: $370–$400
- Restaurant (half-board)
- Swimming pool
- Dogs welcome

LA VILLA ESTELLE Provence

HAUT-DE-CAGNES-SUR-MER 5, montée de la Bourgade, 06800. Tel: 011 33 4 92 02 89 83. Fax: 011 33 4 92 02 88 28. E-mail: estelle@villa-estelle.com

AN EXTREMELY SWANK GUEST HOUSE

In the Provençal backcountry, in the heart of a 12th century village, it took 12 months' hard work for interior decorator Estelle Réale to turn an old inn into a magnificent guest house. The building runs along a terra cotta-floored terrace complete with stone columns from Tunisia and Vallauris pots, overflowing with bougainvillaea and jasmine. This is where guests have their meals. Estelle has designed her villa like a real home. It is fully equipped with living rooms, lounges, a library, and a genuine kitchen with walls covered in a terra cotta-colored, polished rendering. In the office-cum-library that opens onto the terrace, church torchères, set up as lamps, stand beside a 1940 armchair and a 17th century Italian desk-table. The rooms are in pastel shades—pink, green, ochre, light blue—

with creative pieces by the owner confirming her fondness for eclecticism: huge banquettes, small wardrobes and cupboards, remodeled pieces of furniture, which she cuts, transforms or enlarges. This priceless mix of finely-worked furniture and objects from a wide range of places gives this marvellous villa a spirit of conviviality. Estelle Réale has managed to create a place where visitors are welcomed as if by old friends.

HELPFUL INFORMATION
- Open year round, except from 12/22 to 12/28
- 5 minutes from Nice Airport
- Close to Cannes, Nice and Cagnes-sur-Mer train stations
- 5 rooms: $145–$185
- 1 suite: $230
- Prices may vary depending upon the length of the stay
- Dogs welcome

LA BASTIDE DE MOUSTIERS Provence

MOUSTIERS-SAINTE-MARIE Chemin de Quinson, 04360. Tel: 011 33 4 92 70 47 47. Fax: 011 33 4 92 70 47 48. E-mail: contact@bastide-moustiers.com

WHERE THE ART OF GOOD FOOD IS SYNONYMOUS WITH THE ENJOYMENT OF LIFE

"I really fell for Moustiers," chef Alain Ducasse admits, recounting what happened when he was looking for a place where he could receive a few favored clients. "It was love at first sight." With interior designer Tonia Peyrot, he transformed this magnificent residence, which in the 17th century belonged to a master earthenware maker, into a very attractive inn. He brought in local craftsmen to restore some of Moustier's original character and charm. Old furniture and rich fabrics give this friendly inn a rare mix of luxury and simplicity. Alain Ducasse has created an impeccable staging post.

HELPFUL INFORMATION
- Open year round
- 45 minutes from Manosque train station
- 11 rooms :
$150–$260 (low season),
$170–$275 (high season)
- 1 suite:
$260 (low season),
$295 (high season)
- Restaurant
- Swimming pool
- Dogs not allowed

L'HOSTELLERIE Provence

CRILLON-LE-BRAVE Place de l'Église, 84410. Tel: 011 33 4 90 65 61 61. Fax: 011 33 4 90 65 62 86. E-mail: crillonbrave@relaischateaux.fr

HELPFUL INFORMATION
- Open from 3/15 to 1/1
- 90 minutes from Marseille Airport
- 24 rooms: $150–$350
- 8 suites: $270–$510
- Restaurant and bistrot
- Swimming pool
- Dogs welcome

A HAVEN OF COMFORT AT THE FOOT OF MONT VENTOUX

If you want to discover the "real" Provence, spend some time at the Crillon-Le-Brave inn. It is located in the middle of one of the most beautiful scenic areas in the region: the Ventoux mountain, the pinnacles of Montmirail, the Nesque gorges

and the Senanque abbey. This stunning hotel, with its attentive and dedicated staff, and its truly exquisite cuisine, has become part of the network of prestigious hotels in the Relais et Châteaux guide. The ancient Roman theater at Orange is nearby, as are the Isle-sur-la-Sorgue and Carpentras marketplaces, not to mention the remains of Vaison-la-Romaine. For the traveler with an inquiring mind this is an ideal vacation spot.

LA MIRANDE Provence

AVIGNON 4, place de la Mirande, 84000. Tel: 011 33 4 90 85 93 93. Fax: 011 33 4 90 86 26 85. E-mail: mirande@la-mirande.fr

DAINTY ON THE OUTSIDE, SOPHISTICATED ON THE INSIDE

By giving back the identity to this 19th century building, architect François-Joseph Graf has performed a miraculous feat. A large, glassed-in interior courtyard with rattan sofas and chairs is the center of activity for this hotel, where Provençal style is to be found everywhere—in its hexagonal floor tiles, its decorative woodwork and its painted furniture.

HELPFUL INFORMATION
- Open year round
- 2 minutes from Avignon train station
- 19 rooms: $280–$450
- 1 suite: $570–$640
- Restaurant
- Dogs welcome

LE MAS DE PEINT Provence

ARLES Le Sambuc, 13200. Tel: 011 33 4 90 97 20 62. Fax: 011 33 4 90 97 22 20. E-mail: mas-de-peint@avignon-et-provence.com

A STUD FARM IN THE WILD HEARTLAND OF THE CAMARGUE
This cattle estate of grand tradition was built a stone's throw from the sea, on land where horses are still free to run wild. Amongst a herd of some 300 buffalo, there is also, tucked away, a tiny, but exceedingly comfortable hotel, very much in the style of the Camargue. You enter the Mas de Peint through what used to be the stable—the beams of which have been retained for this entrance hall. Meals are taken family style, with everyone gathered around the kitchen table, where the lady of the house prepares free-range chicken, broadbean omelettes, and a garden salad. With its 1,400 acres, this estate is an ideal place for horseback riding, and the perfect setting for those who want to discover and explore the real Camargue.

GRAND HÔTEL NORD PINUS   Provence

ARLES   Place du Forum, 13200. Tel: 011 33 4 90 93 44 44. Fax: 011 33 4 90 93 34 00. E-mail: info@nordpinus.com

UNCONVENTIONALITY AND URBANE GRANDEUR REVIVED

This establishment was founded in the late 19th century and had its moment of glory after World War II. Its owners loved parties and high society, so the Nord Pinus became an obligatory halt for celebrities of all kinds. By keeping the typical features of old-style decoration —wrought iron beds, a tad kitsch, and pastel wall colors— current proprietor Anne Igou has recreated spruce bedrooms with topstitched and quilted fabrics found in the region. In addition, the bathrooms have been enlarged and the bar redecorated based on a bull fighting motif. These new touches have helped the Nord Pinus to regain its urbane splendor and character of yesteryear.

HELPFUL INFORMATION
- Open from 3/2 to 1/14
- 15 minutes from Nîmes Airport
- 5 minutes from Arles train station
- 19 rooms: $125–$166
- 6 suites: $275
- Restaurant (half-board and full-board)
- Dogs welcome

LE CHAUFOURG Périgord

Sourzac 24400. Tel: 011 33 5 53 81 01 56. Fax: 011 33 5 53 82 94 87. E-mail: chaufourg.hotel@wanadoo.fr

A GUEST HOUSE WHERE IT IS A PLEASURE TO TAKE ONE'S TIME

Le Chaufourg was where Georges Dambier spent his boyhood. After the war, he returned to this house, became its proprietor and renovated it with the help of decorators Jean Dive and Janine Dugrenot, and landscape artist Toby Loup de Viane. The result is stunning: light floods into the rooms, marrying the ubiquitous white, which is interrupted by just a few patches of brown from the tiled floors and furniture. The garden, with its box hedges, is an architectural wonder. Visitors cannot help but be spellbound when they spend a few days in this magical guest house, with its newly opened restaurant.

HELPFUL INFORMATION

- Open year round
- 20 minutes from Périgueux and Bergerac airports
- 8 rooms: $142–$236
- 2 suites: starting at $290
- Restaurant
- Swimming pool
- Tennis
- Horseback riding
- Golf
- Dogs welcome in some rooms

LE VIEUX LOGIS Périgord

TRÉMOLAT 24510. Tel: 011 33 5 53 22 80 06. Fax: 011 33 5 53 22 84 89. E-mail: vieuxlogis@relaischateaux.fr

A 17TH CENTURY CHARTERHOUSE BUILT ON THE RUINS OF A PRIORY

Bernard Giraudel has turned his very first holiday home into a hotel devoted to fine living. Maurice Savinel and Roland Le Bévillon, who designed the decor, favored sunny hues. To underscore the soul of this residence, they used Italian-style patinas, antique regional furniture and Souléiado prints. Everything here oozes the poetry of country living. The garden, with its babbling brook, the orchard, and the mighty pyramid-like oak, all invite guests on bucolic walks. The chef is faithful to regional culinary traditions, offering dishes "interpreted" in his own way, making for a dining experience where the great classics live happily alongside cep tart and truffles en papillotte. The hotel is an ideal spot for lovers of tranquillity and nature.

HELPFUL INFORMATION
- Open from 2/12 to 1/1
- 45 minutes from Bergerac Airport
- 18 rooms: $128–$217
- 6 suites: $267
- Restaurant (half-board)
- Swimming pool
- Dogs welcome

LE COUVENT DES HERBES Landes

EUGÉNIE-LES-BAINS 40320. Tel: 011 33 5 58 05 05 05/011 33 5 58 05 06 07. Fax: 011 33 5 58 51 10 10. E-mail: guerard@relaischateaux.fr

AN IDEAL GUEST HOUSE FOR PEOPLE HANKERING AFTER PEACE AND QUIET

This 18th century convent has been turned into a splendid guest house by Christine and Michel Guérard. All the bedrooms—which have their own living rooms—are quite different but have the same color scheme. Today the former convent takes in people who desire calm. It is an ideal haven for those who yearn for that which is "authentic," people who won't balk at walking through the garden to get to the spa and the dining room; even when it is raining. This magical spot is designed for those whose problems will be sorted out by a few days of serenity and sophisticated fare.

HELPFUL INFORMATION

- Open from 2/15 to 12/15
- 45 minutes from Pau Airport
- 4 rooms:
$280 (low season),
$330 (high season),
$360 (in August)
- 4 suites:
$385 (low season),
$450 (high season),
$470 (in August)
- 2 restaurants
- Swimming pool & steam room
- Spa & gym
- Dogs welcome
(with additional charge)

LA FERME AUX GRIVES Landes

Eugénie-Les-Bains 40320. Tel: 011 33 5 58 05 06 07. Fax: 011 33 5 58 51 10 10. E-mail: guerard@relaischateaux.fr

AN HISTORIC INN AMIDST A CHARMING FLOWER GARDEN

In the autumn of 1859, this inn received French empress Eugénie. Today, the inn has regained its reputation for generosity thanks to Christine and Michel Guérard. Fine country cooking spellbinds lovers of golden brown pork and chickens on the spit. Adjoining the grange stands a charming, large house built in 1815, and now very much revived: bull's-eye windows, old stones and terra cotta floors have all regained their former luster. Antique furniture, canopy beds and rich fabrics embellish the bedrooms. In the magnificent garden, the main walk is mapped out by delphiniums, lupines, sage bushes and hardy roses.

HELPFUL INFORMATION
- Open from 2/1 to 12/31
- 45 minutes from Pau Airport
- 1 room: $285 (low season), $330 (high season), $360 (in August)
- 3 suites: $385 (low season), $450 (high season), $470 (in August)
- 2 restaurants
- Swimming pool
- Spa & steam room
- Gym
- Dogs welcome (with additional charge)

LES SOURCES DE CAUDALIE Landes

BORDEAUX-MARTILLAC Chemin de Smith-Haut-Lafitte, 33650. Tel: 011 33 5 57 83 83 53. Fax: 011 33 5 57 83 83 84. E-mail: sources@sources-caudalie.com

HAPPINESS IS A VINEYARD

The new annex at the Sources de Caudalie, la Grange au Bateau, was conceived by architects Collet & Burger, and built using timber retrieved from farms and *maison de maître* (mansions) in the Landes. The building, which is built on the remains of an old cellar, gives the impression of having been enlarged and developed in successive stages. Today, there are three suites and 17 rooms—each with seafaring names like "Les Pagaies," "Le Vent du large," and "Les Régates"—placed alongside the beautiful Smith-Haut-Lafitte vineyards. The owner, Florence Cathiard, was inspired by the waters of Aquitaine for her decoration and makes use of oars, boats, barges, and canoes. In the rooms, she has used quilted bedspreads to add even more comfort to the beds, and has placed linen on the windows and on the seats. In the bathrooms, slate covers the walls and floors. Franck Salein's two restaurants offer local and regional cooking, as well as special meals, low in calories, but not in taste. Often people come here for the Vinotherapy Institute and treatments based on the beneficial properties of the grape.

HELPFUL INFORMATION
- Open year round
- 40 rooms:
$185–$220 (low season),
$215–$250 (high season)
- 9 suites:
$305–$405 (low season),
$365–$450 (high season)
- Gastronomical restaurant and brasserie (half-board and full-board)
- Swimming pool
- Seawater therapy
- Gym
- Dogs welcome
(with additional charge)

LE CHAT BOTTÉ Charentes

ILE DE RÉ Place de l'Église, 17590 Saint-Clément-des-Baleines. Tel: 011 33 5 46 29 21 93. Fax: 011 33 5 46 29 29 97. Website: www.hotelchatbotte.com

A SEASIDE HAVEN OF CALM AND PRIVACY

At the western tip of the Ile de Ré, in Saint-Clément-des-Baleines, this ancient family inn, called Le Chat Botté has been turned into a delightful, small hotel. The renovation of the premises is the combined brain-child of developer Francis Chantreau and the inn's two new owners, Géraldine and Chantal Massé. They have opted for authentic materials such as sand-hued terra cotta for the floors and pale wood for the paneled walls. In the bedrooms, which are each unique, the fabrics are of tender, southerly colors. In the very middle of the hotel, there is a health center where seaweed packs and hot tubs help to turn your stay into a moment of utter rest and relaxation. With its patio and garden, Le Chat Botté is a most welcome and hospitable place.

HELPFUL INFORMATION

- Open from 2/8 to 11/27, and from 12/17 to 1/5
- 45 minutes from La Rochelle train station
- 19 rooms: $63–$98 (low season), $70–$105 (high season)
- Restaurant
- Fitness center
- Dogs welcome (with additional charge)

LA MAISON RICHEUX Bretagne

SAINT-MELOIR-DES-ONDES Le Point du Jour, 35350. Tel: 011 33 2 99 89 25 25. Fax: 011 33 2 99 89 88 47. E-mail: info@maisons-de-bricourt.com

A PEACEFUL HALT IN THE BAY OF MONT-SAINT-MICHEL

In the 1920s, architect Yves Féma built La Maison Richeux on the site called Le Point du Jour. But the establishment's business collapsed at the end of World War II. In 1992, Olivier Roellinger bought it and completely renovated it, much to the delight of his visitors. With its rooms and apartments decorated with English furniture and bright fabrics, today's hotel combines simplicity with perfection. It is also very pleasant to sample and discover here all the magic of the bay of Mont-Saint-Michel. You can actually meditate on the merging of land and sea, while letting the calmness which drives the churning of the tides wash over you. This delightful hotel is well worth the detour. It is particularly recommended for those fond of sweeping landscapes and poetry.

HELPFUL INFORMATION

- Open year round
- 15 minutes from Saint-Malo train station
- 11 rooms:
$160–$267
- 2 suites:
$267–$298
- Restaurant
- Dogs welcome
(with additional charge)

LE GRAND HÔTEL DES BAINS Bretagne

LOCQUIREC 15, rue de l'Église, 29241. Tel: 011 33 2 98 67 41 02. Fax: 011 33 2 98 67 44 60. E-mail: hotel-des-bains@wanadoo.fr

A HANDSOME RESIDENCE WITH EARLY 20TH CENTURY CHARMS

Le Grand Hôtel des Bains calls to mind those great seaside hotels popular with children in the early years of the 20th century. Located in the little fishing village of Locquirec, on the very rim of a red granite coast, the hotel stands on a beautiful promontory. The original building has been redesigned in a manner reminiscent of New England homes—so you will find polished parquet floors, beige and gray paneling, and intricate, white wooden balconies. Every effort has been made to preserve the slightly old-fashioned charm

of the early 20th century. The furniture, decorative objects and prints all come from local antique shops. Comfort is the hallmark throughout the hotel. Your relaxation will be heightened by various health amenities, such as seaweed packs, massages and mud baths.

HELPFUL INFORMATION
- Open from 2/1 to 12/31
- 15 minutes from Morlaix train station
- 36 rooms: $85 (low season), $233 (high season)
- Restaurant (half-board and full-board in July and August)
- Swimming pool
- Seawater therapy
- Jacuzzi and steam room
- Gym
- Dogs welcome (with additional charge)

SCHOLTESHOF Belgium

STEVOORT Kermtstraat 130, 3512, Belgium. Tel: 011 32 11 25 02 02. Fax: 00 32 11 25 43 28. E-mail: scholteshof@relaischateaux.com

**ALL THE ATMOSPHERE OF
A FAMILY HOME WITH
GASTRONOMIC REFINEMENT**

Deep in the countryside, renowned chef Roger Souveyrence has set up his hotel/restaurant in a lovely building that is steeped in history and was once used as the residence of the bailiff of the estate. As the day unfolds, guests can make the most of every room in the house. Prepared at the table, the various dishes are made with the produce from the huge vegetable garden, and the menu offers top-quality specialties. Everyone is free to go and choose their wine from the cellar. The setting is as delightful as the meals: a rose garden, a pond, a botanical garden laid out along medieval lines and a verdant park all invite you to rest or walk. The buzzwords here are warm welcome, subtlety, symbiosis with nature and fine fare.

HELPFUL INFORMATION
- Open from 2/7 to 1/20
- 50 minutes from Brussels-Zaventem Airport
- 60 minutes from Antwerp Airport
- 7 rooms: $100–$150
- 10 suites: $225
- 2 apartments: $350
- Restaurant
- Dogs welcome

ROMANTIK PANDHOTEL Belgium

BRUGES Pandreitje 16, 8000, Belgium. Tel: 011 32 50 34 0666. Fax: 011 32 50 34 0556. E-mail: info@pandhotel.com

ENGLISH STYLE IN AN 18TH CENTURY HOTEL

In the heart of old Bruges, this hotel—which in the 18th century was a large mansion—has been designed, room by room, by somebody with a passion for English decoration. Apart from the use of objects, furniture and fabrics hunted down in London, Chris Vanhaecke has created six suites using differently colored Ralph Lauren fabrics. The refined decor mingles French mirrors with carved frames, 18th century Italian console tables, patinae'd Louis XVI armchairs, and wrought iron four-poster beds. Thanks to Vanhaecke and his two children, the welcome here is all warmth and friendliness. There is no restaurant, but eateries along the canal are many.

HELPFUL INFORMATION

- Open year round
- 70 minutes from Brussels-Zaventem Airport
- 2 minutes from Bruges station
- 15 rooms: $170–$210
- 9 suites: $250–$320
- Dogs welcome

SEVEN ONE SEVEN Netherlands

AMSTERDAM Prinsengracht 717, 1017 JW, Netherlands. Tel: 011 31 20 427 07 17. Fax: 011 31 20 423 07 17. E-mail: info@717hotel.nl

A CANAL-SIDE TROVE OF PRECIOUS OBJECTS

In this 19th century building, Kees van der Valk has created a guest house that combines his gifts as a decorator, fashion designer and men's fashion consultant. The façade is ritzy, if a tad austere, and as soon as you open the door, a superb palette of colors takes your breath away. Pale, sage greens and sea green give way to turquoise, while an infinite range of grays hold their own, and the slate walls perfectly match the charcoal gray flannel curtains. Art objects and furniture from antique shops and boutiques in Brussels and Amsterdam create a thoroughly warm atmosphere and a coziness in the suites. You will find much comfort in this sophisticated setting.

HELPFUL INFORMATION
- Open year round
- 20 minutes from Amsterdam-Schiphol Airport
- 8 suites: $375–$625
- Dogs not allowed

BLAKES Netherlands

AMSTERDAM Keizersgracht 384, 1016 GB, Netherlands. Tel: 011 31 20 530 20 10. Fax: 00 31 20 530 20 30. E-mail: hotel@blakes.nl

COLONIAL ART OF LIVING IN A FORMER 17TH CENTURY THEATER

Anouska Hempel's original idea was to inject these premises with the magic of Holland's colonial past, when fabric merchants plied the seas towards Indonesia. The dominant hues are black, navy blue, reds and greens, and each type of room has a special color scheme: spicy colors, dark blue and white stripes, raspberry, and tropical green. The ground floor with its oriental spirit, includes a long gallery lit by 14 windows and furnished with sofas. As an allusion to its theatrical past, the blinds conjure up stage sets. The restaurant serves western and Asian fare.

HELPFUL INFORMATION

- Open year round
- 30 minutes from Amsterdam-Schiphol Airport
- 23 rooms: $350–$450
- 19 suites: $600–$1,250
- Restaurant
- Dogs not allowed

Haarlem Exclusive Guest Residence, 8 Spaarne, 2011 CH, Netherlands. Tel: 011 31 23 55 11 544. Fax: 011 31 23 53 42 602. E-mail: info@spaarne8.com

TWO ROOMS WITH VERY SPECIAL CHARM

When Peter Schoenmaker opened a hotel in his home in Haarlem, it changed his life. He had a smallish area, so he was restricted to creating just two bedrooms overlooking a pretty garden. His partner, Janneke Muileboom, assumed the task of creating an atmosphere that is at once simple and luxurious: off-white walls, furniture from antique shops, old pine doors found in Antwerp. No fabrics, except those covering the lounge chairs, and the linen blinds warding off prying eyes in the street. The beds sport cozy comforters typical of northern countries. An ideal hotel for discovering Amsterdam and returning at night to a small town with all the relaxing charm of the provinces.

HELPFUL INFORMATION
- Open year round
- 15 minutes from Amsterdam-Schiphol Airport
- 5 minute walk from Haarlem train station
- 2 rooms: $290–$350
- Dogs not allowed

THE PELHAM HOTEL England

LONDON 15, Cromwell Place, SW7 2LA, England. Tel: 011 44 20 7589 8288. Fax: 011 44 20 7584 8444. E-mail: pelham@firmdale.com

COUNTRY HOUSE ATMOSPHERE IN THE HEART OF THE CITY

With its mahogany prints and its homey fabrics, the Pelham Hotel brings together all the elements of British comfort. Kit Kemp, mistress of the house, was keen to give each room a romantic feel. The decoration mixes floral, striped and checked fabrics, woodwork and old drawings. The Pelham offers high-class service, and the luxury of experiencing country privacy in the heart of London.

HELPFUL INFORMATION
- Open year round
- 30 minutes from London Heathrow Airport
- 51 rooms at $235
- 3 suites: $429–$1,077
- Restaurant
- Dogs welcome

CANARY WHARF England

LONDON 46, Westferry Circus, E14 8RS England. Tel: 011 44 20 7510 1999. Fax: 011 44 20 7510 1998. E-mail: sales.caw@fourseasons.com

A CONTEMPORARY SETTING WITH A VIEW OF THE THAMES

Just 10 minutes from Heathrow Airport, the seven-story building that houses the Four Seasons Canary Wharf is a fine example of contemporary architecture—with its copper dome, square windows and mahogany doors. The interior decoration puts the accent on natural, raw materials such as wood, stone and leather. The entrance hall is of spectacular proportions:. It encompasses three levels, with four quite distinctive areas—the concierge's desk, the cloakroom, the salon bar and the reception desk—each of which is designed to resemble a wooden cube shape. The beige hues of the walls are brightened up with touches of black currant. The rooms, in sepia and chocolate-brown tones, are color-coordinated with the cream marble bathrooms, where the glass tiles resemble alabaster. In the intimate and, at the same time lavishly decorated, Italian restaurant, the open kitchen, set in the middle of the dining-room, offers a panoramic view of the cooks at work. But perhaps the most special feature of the hotel lies in its geographical location: a rapidly growing neighborhood on the banks of the Thames, with a sublime view over London's most mythical landmarks.

HELPFUL INFORMATION

- Open year round
- 10 minutes from London Heathrow Airport
- 142 rooms: $406–$484
- 14 suites: $780–$2,341
- Restaurant
- Swimming pool
- Sauna
- Gym
- Little dogs welcome

THE HEMPEL England

LONDON 31-35, Craven Hill Gardens, W2 3EA, England. Tel: 011 44 20 7298 9000. Fax: 011 44 20 7402 4666. E-mail: hotel@the-hempel.co.uk

**BEHIND A GEORGIAN FAÇADE,
A ZEN SPIRIT AND
MINIMALIST DESIGN**

Just north of Hyde Park, the Hempel Hotel stands out from other Georgian houses that all look alike, because of its unexpected oriental and minimalist atmosphere. It overlooks an expanse of lawn with three ponds surrounded by paths of pale gravel that are lined with box bushes and white spheres. What first strikes the eye is the simplicity of materials and colors. Beige for the floors, black and granite for the bathrooms, sand, rust, gray and black for the different floors. Motifs painted directly onto the walls embellish the rooms. Anouska Hempel has here produced a wonderful oeuvre, with a happy mixture of minimalist design and high-tech concept, influenced by the sobriety of the Orient. The hotel is an oasis of peace and calm in the heart of a bustling city.

HELPFUL INFORMATION
- Open year round
- 45 minutes from London Heathrow Airport
- 41 rooms: $398–$460
- 5 apartments: $2,029
- Restaurant
- Dogs welcome

BLAKES England

LONDON 33, Roland Gardens, SW7 3PF, England. Tel: 011 44 20 7370 6701. Fax: 011 44 20 7373 0442. E-mail: blakes@easynet.co.uk

HELPFUL INFORMATION

- Open year round
- 45 minutes from London Heathrow Airport
- 42 rooms: $265–$1,007
- 9 suites: $554
- Restaurant
- Dogs not allowed

EXERCISES IN DECORATIVE STYLES IN KENSINGTON

In the heart of London, Lady Weinberg, owner of the premises, has thought up a different decor for each bedroom: from Biedermeier by way of neo-classicism and grand Russia, to a monastic-like atmosphere with white or raw linen. The attention to detail is meticulous, and everything seems like a stage set. She has chosen a maharajah's bed and marble bowls from Rajasthan for the Indian room, and 19th century silverwork and antique prints for a small Directoire living room. This patchwork of styles forms the setting of a hotel renowned for its impeccable service, which attracts an international jet set. Daring and careful refinement is the hallmark of a lady who loves decoration and invests her all to realize her dreams.

ONE ALDWYCH England

London 1, Aldwych Street, WC2B 4RH, England. Tel: 011 ++ 20 7300 1000. Fax: 011 ++ 20 7300 1001. E-mail: sales@onealdwych.co.uk

MODERN DECOR FOR A FASHIONABLE SPOT

The contemporary and carefully thought out decoration of this luxury hotel attracts an artistic clientele to its location a stone's throw from the City. The wealth of colors and fabrics acts as an enhancing backdrop for 350 artworks. Decorative features peculiar to interior decorator Mary Fox Linton include her use of space, clarity and pure lines. The result is a dazzling success for this hotel located in the Morning Post building.

HELPFUL INFORMATION
- Open year round
- 5 minutes from Waterloo train station
- 40 minutes from London Heathrow Airport
- 93 rooms: $461–$593
- 12 suites: $773–$1,444
- 2 restaurants
- Swimming pool
- Sauna & steam room
- Gym
- Dogs not allowed

COVENT GARDEN England

LONDON 10, Monmouth Street, WC2 9BH, England. Tel: 011 44 20 7806 1000. Fax: 011 44 20 7806 1100. E-mail: covent@firmdale.com

CHARM AND COMFORT IN A TYPICALLY BRITISH, OH-SO-COZY HOTEL

The Covent Garden is one of the most surprising and elegant small hotels in England. Situated in Soho, in the thick of London's busy theater district, it occupies an old 19th century French dispensary. A log fire offers a permanent welcome to visitors in the lounge and library. The spacious rooms have huge windows looking out over the roofs of London. The interior decoration, the work of Kit Kemp, is in the purest English style, with a harmonious mix of materials (wood, stone and steel) as well as styles (ancient and modern). The hand-crafted fabrics come from India and China, and canopies and floral patterns set the typical British tone of the place. Here, carefully selected fabrics, the finest wallpaper and tasteful objects all help to make your stay a most agreeable one. This hotel is proof, if proof were necessary, that the English are indeed experts in the field of comfort. As a population of travelers, they have found the cure for homesickness by lending their hotels a particular charm that allows you to forget how far away you are and feel as if you were in your own home.

HELPFUL INFORMATION

- Open year round
- 45 minutes from London Heathrow Airport
- 58 rooms: $367–$460
- Restaurant
- Gym
- Dogs welcome

LONDON 10, Beaufort Gardens, SW3 1PT, England. Tel: 011 44 20 7584 6300. Fax: 011 44 20 7584 6355. E-mail: knightsbridge@firmdale.com

A VERY SWELL BED-AND-BREAKFAST

Tim and Kit Kemp certainly have a knack for capturing the mood of the times. They have just added a new concept to their Firmdale Hotel chain by creating a deluxe version of the traditional bed-and-breakfast in the heart of the sophisticated Knightsbridge neighborhood. Located in a discreet, secluded square known as Beaufort Gardens—which is a stone's throw from legendary Harrods—the Knightsbridge Hotel offers 44 rooms and suites decorated by Kit Kemp, each with its own personal design. "For some rooms, I wanted soft, neutral colors, while elsewhere I've mixed strong and bold hues," the designer said. There are lots of coordinated materials, and everywhere you look you will find great sophistication in the way curtains and seats are made. On the ground floor, there are two large lounges—one of which is in an African style, with earthy shades, and lots of black and white. The library has managed to retain a romantic feel with its pale pinks and greens. All the walls are hung with original works by contemporary British artists. For his fifth hotel, Kit Kemp has managed to come up with a formula that is at once ritzy and adorable, in one of the famous spots of the capital.

HELPFUL INFORMATION
- Open year round
- 30 minutes from London Heathrow Airport
- 5 minutes from Knightsbridge subway station
- 42 rooms: $211–$382
- 2 suites: $507
- Dogs not allowed

CHARLOTTE STREET England

LONDON 15-17, Charlotte Street, W1T 1RJ, England. Tel: 011 44 20 7806 2000. Fax: 011 44 20 7806 2002. E-mail: charlotte@firmdale.com

HELPFUL INFORMATION

- Open year round
- 50 minutes from London Heathrow Airport
- 44 rooms: $328–$460
- 8 suites: $515–$929
- Restaurant
- Gym
- Dogs not allowed

FINESSE AND COMFORT, ENGLISH-STYLE

Located close to Soho Square—in the heart of the media, theater and fashion districts—the Charlotte Street Hotel is among the most successful of London's hotels of charm. Tim and Kit Kemp have designed a decor of granite and oak adorned with broad-striped wallpaper. This combination goes well with the tiles and the checked or floral patterns of the hand-embroidered quilted bed-spreads that are spread out, invitingly, on the high perched beds. Most of the lights, mirrors and brackets were designed by Kit especially for the hotel. The Kemps have also provided guests with areas to relax in. The hotel features a sports center, a cinema, and a very friendly and popular bar. In the hotel restaurant, dishes are prepared perfectly for waiting gourmets. Lastly, the lounge—its walls adorned with wonderful paintings by Alfred Moulmark and Keith Purser—is still, indisputably, the most comfortable spot in the hotel, with its sofas, welcoming armchairs and tapestry-covered footrests.

LAVENHAM High Street, Sudbury CO10 9QA, England. Tel: 011 44 870 400 8116. Fax: 011 44 17 87 248 286. E-mail: swan1@macdonaldshotels.co.uk

THE MELLOWNESS OF THE ENGLISH COUNTRYSIDE

In Great Britain, the Heritage chain has taken over many history-rich houses, some of which have been redecorated by Ann Boyd, former fashion designer for Ralph Lauren. She

has put her talents to the Swan, located in the Tudor village of Lavenham, which has been known since the 15th century, as a center for wool. This former medieval inn consists of three buildings, offering 41 rooms with four-poster beds, open fires in winter, and 16th and 18th century paintings on the walls. Everything here is poetic and magical—the restaurant with a gallery for the musicians who play daily, the sheltered garden where you can take dinner on summer eves, and the bar, which used to be the haunt of American pilots during World War II (Glen Miller would come here and drink here with his buddies). Around Lavenham, there are several interesting sites: Gainsborough's house at Sudbury, antique shops at Long Melford, and Bury St.Edmund's cathedral, as well as wonderful parks and gardens.

HELPFUL INFORMATION
- Open year round
- 90 minutes from Stan Stead
- 51 rooms: $94–$117
- 4 suites: $124–$156
- Restaurant
- Dogs welcome

LLYSWEN Powys LD3 OYP, England. Tel: 011 44 1 874 754 525. Fax: 011 44 1 874 754 545. E-mail: 101543.3211@compuserve.com

AN OLD WELSH MANOR
TURNED INTO A GUEST-HOUSE

It was on the foundations of an old 17th century manor house that Sir Clough Williams Ellis built this large residence in 1913. A change of scenery in the greatest of comfort is yours at this hotel situated in the Wye valley. Everything has been done to offer you well-being and tranquility. The spacious bedrooms are all decorated with Laura Ashley fabrics, and four-poster beds, authentic Victorian furniture and sublime paintings await you. This elegance, amid sumptuous landscapes, will certainly give you a chance to sample the charm of the Welsh art of living.

HELPFUL
INFORMATION

- Open year round
- 30 minutes from Cardiff Airport
- 20 rooms: $250–$460
- 3 suites: $500–$531
- Restaurant (half-board)
- Tennis
- Croquet
- Fishing

MARFIELD HOUSE Ireland

GOREY Courtown Road, Co Wexford, England. Tel: 011 353 55 21124. Fax: 00 353 55 21572. E-mail: info@marfieldhouse.ie

ANGLO-SAXON COMFORT IN A MANOR HOTEL IN THE WOODS

Marfield House, built in 1820, was purchased by Ray and Mary Bowe in 1977, and transformed into a quality manor hotel. The Bowes have created an extremely refined and luxurious haven. The interior decoration has been reworked throughout —from the antique furniture, fireplaces and Persian carpets, to the bathrooms. Elegant little lounges suddenly appear around the corner of a corridor. This most hospitable world is rounded off by an outstanding restaurant (very well ranked in the Michelin guide), and a dream environment with 30 acres of woodland for sporting guests keen on playing tennis and golf or going horseback riding.

HELPFUL INFORMATION
- Open from 1/1 to 12/15
- 45 minutes from Dublin Airport
- 20 rooms: $240
- 6 suites: $400–$695
- Restaurant
- Sauna
- Dogs welcome

KVIKNE'S HOTEL Norway

BALESTRAND Balholm, 6898, Norway. Tel: 011 47 57 69 42 00. Fax: 011 47 57 69 42 01. E-mail: booking@kviknes.no

ferry service and its location opposite Sogne fjord, overlooked, by only a few rooms, the hotel is busy, summer after summer. The lounge has been luxuriously decorated around furniture made by sculptor Hoyvik.

HELPFUL INFORMATION

- Open from 4/1 to 10/31
- 90 minutes from Sogndal Airport
- 207 rooms: $63 (low season), $93 (high season)
- 11 suites: $104 (low season), $133 (high season)
- Restaurant (half-board)
- Sauna
- Gym
- Dogs not allowed

A CLASSY HOTEL IN THE HEART OF SCANDINAVIAN LANDSCAPES

Once a grocer's store and modest tavern in the early 19th century, Kvikne's became, in just a few decades, the most famous hotel in the Sogndal region. Thanks to

ROISHEIM HOTEL Norway

LOM N-2686, Norway. Tel: 011 47 61 21 20 31. Fax: 110 47 61 21 21 51. E-mail: r-drif-a@roisheim.no

HELPFUL INFORMATION
- Open from 5/15 to 9/31
- 4 1/2 hours from Gardermoen Airport
- 4 1/2 hours from Otta train station
- 24 rooms: $286
- 3 suites: $381
- Restaurant (full-board)
- Dogs welcome

COMFORT AND LUXURY IN A MOUNTAINOUS REGION

After driving along a mountain road that crosses some of Norway's loveliest valleys, at an altitude of 2,100 feet, you will come upon this 12-building old inn housing bedrooms and suites. The main 16th century building is landmarked; the other buildings are chalets dating from the 18th century. The interior decoration reflects mountain comfort and a rustic quality. Four-poster beds and bathrooms with painted wooden paneling predominate. At the Roisheim Hotel, you feel that you are in a real home, with old furniture, a library, gargantuan breakfasts with a wide range of jams, and the outstanding welcome extended by the owners, Ingrid and Haavard Lunde. The food is wonderful, and the wine is delicious. This is an ideal spot for hikers, reigned over by a bracing climate that once inspired previous guests Henrik Ibsen and Edvard Grieg.

HOLMENKOLLEN PARK HOTEL Norway

OSLO Kongevein, 26, N-0787, Norway. Tel: 011 47 22 92 20 00. Fax: 011 47 22 14 61 92. E-mail: holmenkollen.park.hotel.rica@rica.no

A ROOM WITH A VIEW
OVER THE CAPITAL

With a superb view over Oslo, the Holmenkollen Park Hotel Rica is a favorite weekend hang-out of the capital's citizenry. In this former sanatorium, which survived a terrible fire in 1914, you will find lounges, dining-rooms and venues for seminars, done up with beautiful oil paintings, and antique furniture. A sumptuous wooden stairway leads to the upper floors in the old part of the hotel. The 150 rooms take up the modern wing, designed in 1982, which has turned out to be a major architectural success. The quality of the food is excellent, and is yet another feature that makes this hotel the place to stay before heading off to the Sogndal region.

HELPFUL INFORMATION

- Open from 1/2 to 12/22
- 45 minutes from Oslo airport
- 220 rooms: $149 (low season), $231(high season)
- 11 suites: $299–$1,088 (low season), $374–$1,905 (high season)
- 2 restaurants
- Swimming pool & sauna –
- Gym
- Dogs welcome

HOTEL MUNDAL Norway

FJÆRLAND N-6848, Norway. Tel: 011 47 57 69 31 01. Fax: 011 47 69 31 79. E-mail: hotelmundal@fjordinfo.no

A WARM HOTEL IN THE NORWEGIAN CHILL

Situated at the foot of the Jostedal glacier, the Mundal has been a major tourist attraction in Norway for many years. At the outset, it was a small guest house run by Mike Mundal, a famous guide in the 20th century who used it to provide refuge to mountaineers, artists and, at times, members of the royal family. Then, the hotel could only be accessed by boat. The hotel has met with great success, and has grown thanks to the construction of a road hewn out beneath the glacier. Built entirely of timber, the Mundal has the old-fashioned charm of a family home with a pool table, a hundred-year-old piano and ancestral portraits. A slightly chaotic brand of comfort, made up for by the warm welcome extended by the owners, who carry on the family tradition.

HELPFUL INFORMATION
- Open from 5/15 to 9/15
- 45 minutes from Sogndal Airport
- 30 rooms: $163–$204
- Restaurant (half-board)
- Dogs welcome

HOTEL DORINT Germany

BERLIN Charlottenstrasse 50-52, 10117, Germany. Tel: 011 49 30 203 750. Fax: 00 49 30 203 75 100

UNPRETENTIOUS, SOBER, SOPHISTICATED LUXURY

Not far from the Brandenburg Gate, the Hotel Dorint has undergone far-reaching changes thanks to architects Harald Klein and Bert Haller. The purest of materials have pride of place: glass, steel and marble. The walls are white, and the furniture has been designed by famous Italian decorators such as Moroso and Minotti. The breakfast room is located in the high-design and very white setting of the "Atrium Café," which goes with the reception foyer. The bedrooms play with space, whiteness and light. Beneath the roofs, the gym and relaxation centers are surrounded by a terrace offering visitors an extraordinary view of the whole city.

HELPFUL INFORMATION

- Open year round
- 30 minutes from Berlin Airport
- 70 rooms:$209–$304
- 22 suites: $275–$600
- Restaurant
- Sauna & steam room
- Gym
- Dogs welcome

HÔTEL D'ANGLETERRE Switzerland

GENEVA 117, quai du Mont-Blanc, 1201, Switzerland. Tel: 011 41 22 906 55 55. Fax: 00 41 22 906 55 56. E-mail: angleterre@rchmail.com

INTIMACY IN A MODERNIZED VICTORIAN STYLE

The D'Angleterre opened its doors in 1872, and accommodated many European crowned heads within its walls. After the Evian Agreement, the establishment went a bit downhill. But once it was renovated, the hotel offered all the comforts that a demanding clientele is entitled to expect. By combining Victorian warmth with distinguished French classicism, interior decorator Anne-Marie de Ganay has managed to recreate a typical 19th century look and feel. In the rooms, bedrooms and suites, the walls are covered with striped damask and Indian fabric. Antique prints, heavy curtains, patterned carpets and mahogany furniture happily emphasize a fidelity to 19th century style.

HELPFUL INFORMATION

- Open year round
- 15 minutes from Geneva Cointrin Airport
- 5 minutes from Cornavin train station
- 39 rooms: $320–$605
- 6 suites: $673–$3,808
- Restaurant
- Sauna
- Gym
- Little dogs admitted upon request

TORRE DI BELLOSGUARDO Italy

FLORENCE Via Roti Michelozzi, 2, 50124, Italy. Tel: 011 39 055 2298145, Fax: 110 39 055 229008. E-mail: info@torredibellosguardo.com

A 13TH CENTURY HOUSE ON THE FLORENTINE HEIGHTS

This spot has the advantage of combining all the most beautiful things Tuscany can offer. Azaleas, magnolias, lemon trees, the deep blue water of the pool, setting off the Gothic windows and carved ceilings, extend their welcome to lovers of beautiful Italy—a permanent delight.

HELPFUL INFORMATION
- Open year round
- 20 minutes from Florence Airport
- 8 rooms: $280
- 7 suites: $330–$380
- Swimming pool
- Sauna
- Dogs welcome

GALLERY HOTEL ART Italy

FLORENCE Vicolo Dell'Oro n° 5, 50123, Italy. Tel: 011 39 055 27263. Fax: 011 39 055 268557. E-mail: gallery@lungarnohotels.it

IN OLD FLORENCE, FLAWLESSLY TASTEFUL MINIMALISM

A stone's throw from the Ponte Vecchio, wedged between two narrow alleyways, a small, modern building of seven floors houses the Gallery Hotel Art. Architect Michele Banane was entrusted with the interior decoration. Though minimalist aesthetics prevail, the lounge-cum-library in wenge wood and velvet has been designed like the library in some old English club. In the morning, you can have breakfast here on low tables, a bit like at home. As for the bedrooms, the style is determinedly masculine, and luxury peeps through in the materials: wood, leather and steel. Views of Florence by

Giampietro Favero embellish the walls of each room, as the Gallery Hotel Art is also a venue where art has its own place. Gallery owner Isabel Brancolini actually makes appointments here with lovers of contemporary art, by way of exhibitions that change on a regular basis.

HELPFUL INFORMATION
- Open year round
- 25 minutes from Florence Airport
- 60 rooms: $265–$350
- 5 suites: $455–$575
- Restaurant
- Dogs welcome

LA POSTA VECCHIA Italy

ROME Località Palo Laziale, 00055 Ladispoli, Italy. Tel: 011 39 06 99 49501. Fax: 011 39 06 99 49507. E-mail: info@lapostavecchia.com

LUXURY AND ROMAN REMAINS IN A DREAM HOTEL

In the 15th century, not far from Rome, Prince Odescalchi built this impressive castle overlooking the Mediterranean. A former residence of the Getty family, this castle—where Roman mosaics, remains and objects dating from the 2nd century B.C. were found—has become a ritzy hotel. The decoration is refined, and it includes veritable archaeological treasures scattered here, there and everywhere. A superb garden and a terrace overlooking the sea enable visitors to sample that Italian dolce vita. Another treasure of the house is its excellent cuisine.

HELPFUL INFORMATION

- Open from 4/12 to 11/3
- 25 minutes from Rome Airport
- 9 rooms: $348–$512
- 8 suites: $775–$1,240
- Restaurant
- Swimming pool
- Sauna
- Gym
- Dogs not allowed

VILLA FIORDALISO Italy

GARDONE RIVIERA Corso Zanardelli, 150, 25083, Italy. Tel: 011 39 0365 20158. Fax: 011 39 0365 290011. E-mail: fiordaliso@relaischateaux.com

A VILLA ON LAKE GARDA

This neo-classical villa, whose construction in the early 20th century took almost 15 years, is nothing less than a gem. An original feature about this holiday place is that it is haunted by historical and poetic memories of the turn of the century. In fact, the poet D'Annunzio once lived here. Today, you cannot stop yourself from gazing in admiration at the beautiful mosaics, the stucco features, the frescoes, the all-marble staircase and the sublime parquet floors that embellish this villa. In addition, all the bedrooms have their original furnishings. With its marble walls and frescoes, the hall opens onto the lake and the gardens, where cypress grows majestically amongst pines, palms and oleander. Sublimeness is achieved when beneath the white awning, gazing out at the lake, you sample the delicious cuisine of the young chef Riccardo Caminini. It is truly a paradise for romantic souls.

HOTEL CIPRIANI Italy

VENICE Giudecca, 10, 30133, Italy. Tel: 011 39 041 5207744. Fax: 011 39 041 5207745. E-mail: info@hotelcipriani.it

HELPFUL INFORMATION

- Open year round
- 30 minutes from Venice-Marco Polo Airport
- 103 rooms: $767–$1,177
- 57 suites: $1,588–$7,588
- 2 restaurants
- Swimming pool
- Sauna
- Gym
- Tennis
- Little dogs welcome

REFINEMENT AND A MAGICAL VIEW OF THE LAGUNE

The Palazzetto, built in the 16th century, seems to be straight out of a Guardi or Canaletto painting. It has one of the finest views over the Doges' Palace and St. Mark's square. The atmosphere echoes the place in a manner that is both sophisticated and elegant. Fortuny fabrics introduce a classy touch to the walls, with their interplay of blue and yellow pastel shades. The furniture is mainly Venetian in inspiration. The restaurant offers high quality fare on its floating terrace. A stay in this magical palace, where hundreds of bells awake you and where the windows overlook the Campanile and the Salute, is a moment of sheer joy.

QUINTA DA CAPELA Portugal

SINTRA Estrada Velha de Colares, P 2710-405, Portugal. Tel: 011 351 219 290 170. Fax: 011 351 219 293 425. E-mail: quintadacapela@hotmail.com

AN OASIS OF GREENERY IN THE PORTUGUESE HILLS

Located in the hills north of Lisbon, within easy reach of the Atlantic beaches, Quinta da Capela is a small hamlet of houses clustered around an impressive monastery-like building. There is an austere simplicity here that heightens the nobility of the place. Old furniture and discreetly arching ceilings are the only decorations. Terraces offer contemplative views over the garden and the verdant landscape surrounding the hotel. Lastly, your stay will be enhanced by the hotel's only concessions to modernity: a gym, a sauna and a pool. The hotel is truly an oasis of calm where the soft scents of wax polish and eucalyptus mingle.

HELPFUL INFORMATION

- Open from 3/1 to 10/31
- 45 minutes from Lisbon Airport
- 15 minutes from Sintra train station
- 8 rooms: $160
- 1 suite: $195
- 3 cottages: $160
- Swimming pool
- Sauna
- Dogs allowed upon request

CASA DE CARMONA Spain

SEVILLE Plaza de Lasso, 1, Carmona, 41410, Spain. Tel: 011 34 95 419 1000. Fax: 011 34 95 419 0189. E-mail: reserve@casadecarmona.com

A MOORISH PATIO JUST A FEW MINUTES FROM SEVILLE

Not far from Cordoba, the Bay of Cadiz and the gardens of the Alhambra, the Casa de Carmona has opened its doors to visitors wishing to spend a few days in a place that is at once historic and comfortable. Thanks to major renovation efforts, this ancient palace has reinstated its gold spangled ceilings, and the colonnades of its huge patio. Great comfort reigns throughout, especially in the typically British bedrooms. As with the bathrooms—where tubs on lion's feet rub shoulders with 1900s sinks—the whole effect of the bedroom results in a happy mix of modernism and traces of yesteryear.

HELPFUL INFORMATION
- Open year round
- 15 minutes from Seville Airport
- 30 rooms: $132–$180 (low season), $138–$204 (high season)
- 1 suite: $481 (low season), $541 (high season)
- Restaurant
- Swimming pool
- Sauna
- Gym
- Dogs welcome

JNANE TAMSNA **Morocco**

MARRAKESH Douar Abiad, La Palmeraie, 40000. Tel: 011 212 44 32 93 40. Fax: 011 212 44 32 98 84. E-mail: info@tamsna.com

HELPFUL INFORMATION

- Open year round
- 25 minutes from Marrakesh Menara Airport
- 10 rooms: $386 (low season), $439 (high season)
- 5 suites-bungalows:
$526 (low season), $604 (high season)
- Restaurant (half-board and full-board)
- 3 swimming pools
- Gym
- Dogs welcome

A COUNTRY HOUSE IN THE MARRAKESH PALM GROVE

Meyrianne Loum-Martin's guest house in the Marrakesh palm grove has 10 rooms arranged around two patios. The first is fragrant with wisteria, jasmine and datura, the latter is planted with olives and artichokes around a fountain. Styles are blended throughout. The bedroom walls are painted in colors associated with English country houses—celadon green, lime, sky-blue, pale yellow and pinkish-beige. The furnishings have been unearthed here and there—a Syrian banquette, a 1940s armchair, an English foot-stool—or like the wrought iron beds and cedar wardrobes custom-built. All the walls are decorated with a collection of old photos featuring oriental themes, as well as with watercolors and oils framed by Séverine Chaperot. The owners have been keen to recreate the spirit of the place as it was some 20 years ago, so they have planted more than a hundred varieties of cereal and vegetables. Meryianne's house really is an authentic country home.

AMANJENA Morocco

MARRAKESH Route de Ourzazate, km 12, 40000. Tel: 011 212 44 40 33 53. Fax: 011 212 44 40 34 77. E-mail: amanjena@amanresorts.com

A MOORISH FEEL, UPDATED

Architect Ed Tuttle designed the plans for this magnificent hotel for the Amanresorts group. His inspiration was the Alhambra, in Grenada, but the materials used were those available in Morocco: rammed earth, tadlakt, and zelliges. The villas, pavilions and houses that make up the complex are built around a square expanse of water that was used for irrigating the palm grove in the 13th century. The complex extends over 17 acres of land, complete with a golf course and olive orchard. Small canals criss-cross the grounds and fountains spout on every terrace, lending an exquisite sensation of coolness. Each pavilion, like a cube with vaulted ceiling, overlooks the pool by way of a covered terrace with huge banquettes and wrought iron furniture. The carpets, rugs and lamps in each of the rooms come from neighboring souks. Fireplaces remind us that it is cold in Marrakesh between the months of November and February. Ed Tuttle, who has designed 40 hotels throughout the world, is fond of saying that

HELPFUL INFORMATION

• Open year round
• 15 minutes from Marrakesh Menara Airport
• 40 suites:
$700–$2,000 (low season),
$800–$2,200 (high season)
• 2 restaurants
• Swimming pool
• Steam room
• Sauna
• Gym
• Dogs not allowed

this one was one of his most demanding challenges and one that took the longest to see the light of day. He succeeded in meeting the challenge. Never has a place better deserved the name of Amanjena: "Aman" meaning peace, and "Jena" meaning paradise.

LA MAISON ARABE Morocco

MARRAKESH 1, Derb Assehbé, Bab Doukkala, 40000. Tel: 011 212 44 38 70 10. Fax: 011 212 44 38 72 21. E-mail: maisonarabe@iam.net.ma

TRADITIONAL DECORATION, AUTHENTICITY AND HOSPITALITY

La Maison Arabe, which used to be a famous restaurant, has, at the hands of Fabrizio Ruspoli, become an enchanting hotel and a real testimony to oriental living of yore. Great attention has been paid to detail. The bedrooms, with terraces like gardens, no less, offer a sense of well-being: antique furniture, orientalist pictures, hand-crafted fabrics, wooden and wrought iron moucharabies, tadlakt walls, warm-hued cedar ceilings, bejmat floors and cupolas letting the light filter in. Guests often enjoy dinner in the restaurant next door.

HELPFUL INFORMATION

- Open year round
- 10 minutes from Marrakesh Menara Airport
- 6 rooms:
$130–$186 (low season),
$158–$214 (high season)
- 7 suites:
$214–$446 (low season),
$260–$558, (high season)
- Restaurant
- Swimming pool
- Steam room
- Dogs not allowed

LA VILLA MAROC Morocco

ESSAOUIRA 10, rue Abdellah Ben Yassine, 44000. Tel: 011 212 44 47 61 47. Fax: 011 212 44 47 58 06. E-mail: hotel@villa-maroc.com

HELPFUL INFORMATION

- Open year round
- 12 rooms:
$70 (breakfast included),
$99 (half-board)
- 6 mini-suites:
$88 (breakfast included),
$118 (half-board)
- 2 suites:
$107 (breakfast included),
$137 (half-board)
- 1 apartment:
$139 (breakfast included),
$ 201 (half-board)
- Restaurant
- Little dogs welcome

A VILLA MADE FOR ORIENTAL DREAMING

It was a certain James who had the bright idea of buying two 18th century riyads and turning them into a delightful guest house, with whitewashed walls and simple, lovely furnishings. Here in a peaceful atmosphere where refinement mingles with aesthetics we find a harmony of typically oriental colors—white and blue reign, right down to the pottery on the floor. In this home, where you are taken in like friends, particular care is given to the service and the food.

NGORONGORO CRATER LODGE Tanzania

ARUSHA Ngorongoro Conservation Area, P.O. Box 751. Reservations: www.ccafrica.com

ON THE EDGE OF ONE OF THE WORLD'S OLDEST VOLCANOES, A CRAZILY LUXURIOUS HOTEL

Not far from Mount Kilimanjaro, and right on the rim of a 3-million-year-old crater, stands an amazing lodge at an altitude of 7,875 feet. Silvio Rech, Chris Browne and 450 Tanzanians took a year to complete this project. From the vast buildings to the tiniest decorative details, absolutely everything was designed and manufactured on the spot. The nearby island of Zanzibar, deeply influenced by the Indian and Arabic arts, inspired the woodwork. Because the place is determinedly Baroque, and intoxication comes from mixing things, Africa here opens its doors to English, Oriental and even Italian influences. The incredible lounge has a Venetian chandelier, delicate porcelain and plenty of mirrors. In the carefully decorated bedrooms, walls and beds are made of *mnenga* wood and the parquet floors of mokoro. You can see and admire the crater from everywhere. When night falls, Maasai in their traditional dress, spears in their hands, escort you to the dining room. In the morning, the moment of breakfast verges on the sublime, when thousands of pink flamingoes take off with the rising sun.

FINCH HATTONS SAFARI CAMP Kenya

NAIROBI P.O. Box 24423. Tel: 011 254 2 310335. Fax: 011 254 2 217778. E-mail: finchhattons@icconnect.co.ke

A CHIC CAMP IN THE THICK OF THE SAVANNAH

Thanks to Peter Frank, you can sample the charm of life in the wild while staying in a chic camp. The handful of comfortable tents are built on stilts and protected by palm roofs. The furnishings are sober: mosquito nets, Victorian lamps, Arabic rugs and chests. Not far away, you can observe the wildlife without risking any danger. In the communal "great hut," there is an English bar with old prints, an impressive dining-room, paintings and crystal ware. On the terrace, you will sample refined dishes as you watch crocodiles yawning and multi-colored birds performing their ballet.

HELPFUL INFORMATION
- Open year round
- 6 hours from Nairobi Airport, then 10 minutes from Finch Hattons runway
- 35 rooms: $285 (low season), $370 (high season)
- Restaurant (full-board)
- Swimming pool
- Dogs not allowed

BORONA Kenya

NAIROBI Borona Rnahc, PO. Box 42730. Tel: 011 254 2 568804. Fax: 011 254 2 564495.

WILD STYLE AND ROUGH FURNITURE IN THE BUSH

From this camp covering some 50,000 acres, you can admire Africa for as far as the eye can see. Surveying a water hole, where elephants come to drink in the evening, this place, with its handful of tents, has been designed so as not to upset the environment. The main great hut is built with large blocks of stone, wood, and palms for the roof. The decoration is typically African: pottery, basketry, tribal fabrics and painted gourds decorate the rooms. All the huts allow the guests to observe the wildlife from afar, and face a superb valley in which a Masai guard keeps permanent vigil.

HELPFUL INFORMATION

- Open year round
- 15 minutes from Nanyuki Airport
- Rooms: starting at $500
- Swimming pool
- Dogs not allowed

KIWAYU Kenya

KIWAYU Safari Village, PO. Box 55343. Tel: 011 254 2 503030. Fax: 011 254 2 503149. E-mail: info@kiwayu.com

A GILDED EDEN FOR APPRENTICE ROBINSON CRUSOES

Alfredo and Lisa Pelizzoli have built a dream hotel, ideal for those who want to pose as Tarzan for a moment. Bungalows surveying nature and ocean alike, and built in the local style, await you by the lagoon and close to two beautiful white, sandy beaches. Coconut palm and mangrove have been used for construction. Under the palm roof, a huge verandah, a bedroom and a bathroom, with floors and walls clad with woven palm, act as your accommodations.

HELPFUL INFORMATION

- Open from 7/30 to 4/15
- 2 hours from Nairobi Airport
- 15 minutes from Lamu track
- 5 minutes from Kiwayu track
- 20 bungalows:
$636 (low season),
$1,100 (high season)
- Restaurant (full-board)
- Windsurfing
- Sailing
- Waterskiing
- Dogs welcome

SINGITA South Africa

BENMORE PO. Box 650881, 2010. Tel: 011 27 11 234 0990. Fax: 011 27 11 234 0535. E-mail: singita@relaischateaux.com

A VERANDAH-SIZED BALCONY ABOVE THE BUSH

Before becoming South Africa's most exclusive lodge, Singita was a private house in the middle of the bush. So, today, this lodge is not only a beautiful feat of decoration, but also a place with a soul. The main house, soaring over the bush, has been converted into a large lounge that overlooks a verandah. The chalet suites are scattered in a verdant garden. Here, romanticism combines with the love of nature, as you can explore the 35,000-acre estate by jeep, and observe the wildlife.

HELPFUL INFORMATION

- Open year round
- 15 minutes from Singita's private airstrip
- 18 bungalows: $473
- Restaurant (full-board)
- Pool in each bungalow
- Spa & gym
- Dogs not allowed

MATETSI GAME LODGES Zimbabwe

VICTORIA FALLS Zambezi River, Nr Victoria Falls. Reservations: Tel: 011 27 11 809 4300. Fax: 011 27 11 809 4400. Email: matetsi@slh.com

AN EXQUISITE ISLAND OF TEAK IN A RESERVE

The Matetsi Game Lodges is a 125,000-acre reserve. There are no fence posts nor any barbed wire to disturb the land. Giraffe, lion, buffalo and elephant all come and go as they wish. Thanks to decorator Sandi Bernstein, everything exudes harmony and purity. You can get delightfully lost in this world of teak. The symbiosis between the land of Africa and the decoration is a total success, and those looking to admire the life of bush animals will surely get their money's worth.

HELPFUL INFORMATION

- Open year round
- 45 minutes from Victoria Falls Airport
- 30 minutes from Victoria Falls train station
- 12 rooms at Safari Camp and

18 rooms at Water Lodge:
$330 (low season),
$400 (high season)
- Restaurant (full-board)
- Swimming pool
- Dogs not allowed

ROYAL PALM Mauritius

GRAND BAIE. Tel: 011 230 209 8300. Fax: 011 230 263 8455. E-mail: royalpalm@bchot.com

LUXURY AND SERENITY BESIDE THE OCEAN

Located at Grand Baie, a small fishing village, the Royal Palm is a veritable oasis, sheltered from stormy winds and endowed with a peerless view over the sea. The sense of serenity is also largely due to the quality of the ubiquitous but discreet service—supervised by director Jean-Pierre Chaumard—and the culture of Mauritius, which combines a sense of welcome with one of refinement. The chef will delight you with flavorful dishes. The whiteness of the sand, the transparency of the sea, the quality of the food and the kindness of the staff give guests the feeling of paradise rediscovered, and provide a setting that is quite difficult to leave.

HELPFUL INFORMATION
- Open year round
- 60 minutes from Sir Seewoosagur International Airport
- 57 rooms: $635–$970
- 27 suites: $1,238–$3,380
- 3 restaurants
- Swimming pool
- Sauna
- Steam room
- Gym
- Dogs not allowed

THE RESIDENCE Mauritius

BELLE MARE Coastal Road. Tel: 011 230 401 88 88. Fax: 011 230 415 58 88. E-mail: reservation@theresidence.com

LUXURY, TRANQUILITY AND EXQUISITE PLEASURE

Here, as you rest on a divine beach with sand plunging into the limpid waters of the Indian Ocean, you will be courteously brought a bottle of mineral water and a slice of fresh watermelon. The hotel is completely sea-oriented and encircled by magnificent gardens. The interior decoration has been designed to be in perfect harmony with the tranquility of this life of luxury in laziness. It is a luminous world, full of cream and white. The bedrooms are decorated in a meticulous way, with carefully appointed bathrooms where wood, stone and gray marble create a harmonious marriage. Potpourris of spices, candles and flowers, combined with the perfect cooking of French chef Benoît Pépin, make this place a delight for all the senses.

HELPFUL INFORMATION
- Open year round
- 50 minutes from Sir Seewoosagur International Airport
- 151 rooms: $325–$850
- 20 suites: $350–$1,823
- 3 restaurants (half-board)
- Swimming pool
- Sauna & steam room
- Spa
- Gym
- Dogs not allowed

THE FRÉGATE ISLAND Seychelles

FRÉGATE ISLAND P.O. Box 330, Victoria Mahé. Tel: 203 602 0300. Fax: 203 602 2265. E-mail: rmiresorts@juno.com

A GARDEN OF EDEN, FOR BEING MAROONED IN STYLE

A private island of just over one square mile, hemmed by seven beaches and buried in tropical vegetation, houses just one hotel. On Frégate Island, there are 16 bungalows, each including a huge living room, a bedroom and two bathrooms. Woodwork, Thai silks and Egyptian cotton create a gentle atmosphere. Large windows offer sublime views over the sea and the archipelago. The pleasures of the world's loveliest beaches go hand in hand with delightful walks in an outstanding setting. Countless varieties of trees —eucalyptus, banyan, coconut palm and mango—are present. Hundred-year-old tortoises live in the forest, along with an infinite variety of amazing birds, such as the cardinal, the gray turtle dove, and fairy terns.

HELPFUL INFORMATION

- Open year round
- 20 minutes from Mahé Island airport
- 16 villas: $1,700
- 2 restaurants (full-board)
- Swimming pool
- Gym
- Dogs not allowed

LEMURIA RESORT Seychelles

PRASLIN ISLAND Anse Kerlan, Praslin. Tel: 011 230 415 1515. Fax: 011 23 415 1082. E-mail: lemuria@seychelles.net

LIKE A DREAM

The Lemuria is a very swank hotel. It was built in 1999 on Praslin Island in the Seychelles, in the heart of a 375-acre palm grove. Its architecture successfully unites wood, open stone, pink granite, marble, thatch and natural fabrics. Between shade and sun, lagoon and palm, the hotel is an enclave of relaxation and allows your thoughts to take flight. The hotel offers 96 suites extended by a broad, shady terrace tastefully decorated. The bathrooms are veiled by slatted, wooden shutters resembling inner patios and separated from the bedrooms by studded shutters. The floors of the bedrooms and the dining rooms are made of sandstone, a type of marble used in tropical countries. This hotel boasts several restaurants. One of them overlooks the two beaches at Kerlan Cove. For dinner, there is a slight preference for La Légende, the main room above the garden. It has comfortable banquettes with scatter cushions and torchères made of teak and leather that are designed, like all the stools, by Martin Branner. With its teak balustrade and its latania roof, it surveys the first of three pools designed like stairs. Clear water trickles down the steps and converges in the pools, which merge with the lagoon in a welter of blue, just like in the movies—or in your dreams.

HELPFUL INFORMATION

- Open year round
- 10 minutes from Praslin Airport
- 80 Junior suites: $300 (low season), $675 (high season)
- 8 Senior suites: $600 (low season), $1,350 (high season)
- 3 restaurants (half-board)
- Swimming pools
- Steam room & sauna
- Dogs not allowed

AMARVILAS RESORT India

AGRA Taj East Gate Road, 282001. Tel: 011 91 562 231515. Fax: 011 91 562 231516. E-mail: gmsecretary@amarvilas.com

A PALACE FIT FOR THE HEROES OF "THE 1,001 NIGHTS"

The Amarvilas hotel is located less than half a mile from one of the world's most beautiful monuments, the Taj Mahal. Most of its rooms have private terraces that provide views of the magnificent mausoleum. This handsome hotel is the work of Bombay architect Patki. The rooms are in Burmese teak, with bathrooms of green marble, giving the hotel very much the look of a palace standing proudly amongst Moghul gardens. The swimming pool, one-third of its length under cover, overlooks espalier gardens where firefly-like lights switch on at nightfall and are reflected in the water. Fountains designed by William Bill Bensley enliven this dream-like setting, beyond which, at dawn, you will glimpse domes emerging from the mist, and, at dusk, glinting in the setting sun.

HELPFUL INFORMATION

- Open year round
- 20 minutes from Agra train station
- 98 rooms: $350–$370
- 7 suites: $800–$2,000
- 2 restaurants
- Swimming pool
- Sauna & spa
- Dogs not allowed

DEVI GARH India

UDAIPUR P.O. Box 144, 313001, Rajasthan. Tel: 011 91 2953 89211. Fax: 011 91 2953 89357. E-mail: reservations@deviresorts.com

AN ENCHANTING HOTEL IN A SUPERB 18TH CENTURY FORT

A few years ago, the Poddar family bought this fort located just 40 minutes from the city of Udaipur. They turned it into a sumptuous 30-room hotel (including seven tents and 23 suites), and used two Indian architects for the conversion and decoration. Both architects were chosen because of their fondness for simple, clean lines. The walls are in chempest, a kind of local waxed rendering. The floors are marble, and the furniture teak. There are no curtains on the windows, but white cotton predominates on the beds, sofas and chairs. The only colors are those of the cushions and the many pictures. The rooms are simple, but extremely elegant.

Meals are taken around the pool, in the different gardens, on the roofs, and even in the dining room. Despite the large staff, made up of 120 people bustling hither and dither, the family makes sure that it personally welcomes every client and visitor.

RAJVILAS India

JAIPUR Goner road, 302004, Rajasthan. Tel: 011 91 141 680 101. Fax: 011 91 141 680 202. E-mail: reservations@rajvilas.com

AN INDIAN PALACE IN THE PUREST MOGHUL TRADITION

It was at Rajvilas, deep in Rajasthan, that the maharajahs formally built their palaces and forts. This hotel concentrates the very best of the moghul style. The main fort is covered, in the traditional way, with a type of rammed clay. On the floor, there is marble inlaid with lapis-lazuli and turquoise, and blue tiles that have been famous since the 19th century. Some bedrooms, like those used by Indian princes

HELPFUL INFORMATION

- Open year round
- 20 minutes from Jaipur Airport
- 53 rooms: $370–$450
- 14 deluxe tents: starting at $450
- 3 villas with swimming pools: $750–$1,500
- Restaurant
- Swimming pool
- Sauna & spa

- Tennis
- Croquet
- Dogs not allowed

on their travels, have been done up beneath sumptuous tents, pitched in a rather arid setting, which contrasts with the hotel's luxuriant gardens.

THE STRAND Burma (Myanmar)

RANGOON 92, Strand Road, Myanmar. Tel: 011 951 2433 77. Fax: 011 951 2898 80. E-mail: strand.ygn@strandhotel.com.mm

ONE OF THE MYTHICAL HOTELS OF MODERNIZED SOUTHEAST ASIA

Located in Rangoon, this hotel, which was built in 1901, was featured in turn of the century guides as "the best hotel east of Suez." Renovated in the 1930s' style, today it once again offers exceptionally comfortable rooms. With its large wooden fans, its rattan chairs and mahogany-slatted blinds, the decoration harmoniously conjures up the colonial atmosphere.

HELPFUL INFORMATION
- Open year round
- 50 minutes from Myanmar International Airport
- 32 suites:
Superior: $415
Luxury: $475
Strand Suite: $900
- Restaurant
- Dogs not allowed

SIEM REAP River Road. Tel: 011 855 63 963 390. Fax: 011 855 63 963 391. E-mail: angkor@pansea.com

THE KHMER TRADITION REVISITED

The wonderful hotel at Siem Reap is inspired by architectural refinements in the Cambodian tradition. It stands close to legendary and mythical temples, upon which the jungle daily closes in. It is not far from Angkor, a veritable "tropical Atlantis," and a forest of stones where architectural master-pieces, mountains, temples and bas-reliefs, swaying to the rhythm of Apsara dancers, go on for a distance of almost 250 miles. Here, in the heart of the colonial quarter, on the water course, is a superb hotel of charm: the Pansea Angkor. Two buildings clad in stone, brick and timber offer 54 bedrooms with views either over the Siem Reap River, or over the swimming pool, in its cocoon of tropical gardens planted with 40 species of trees. The decoration is drawn from Khmer tradition. Architect Guillaume Cochin has used dark-colored tiles in keeping with the gray deck made of persimmon wood—which starts off yellow and becomes gray as it ages. The roof is made of kiln-fired ceramic tiles. In the rooms, mosquito nets are held in place by silk-weaving handles and the furniture, designed by the Amedeo Workshop, is made of

HELPFUL INFORMATION
- Open year round
- 15 minutes from Siem Reap Airport
- 55 rooms: $200–$280
- 1 suite: $350
- Restaurant (half-board)
- Swimming pool
- Dogs not allowed

doungchen, a wood that is softer than teak and thus easier to work. The hotel restaurant, run by the French chef Pierre Vedel, is surrounded by a pond. Blinds on all the windows, which are often left open to keep the air circulating, bring out the colonial look.

AMANPURI Thailand

PHUKET P.O. Box 196, Pansea Beach, 83000. Tel: 011 66 76 324 333. Fax: 011 66 76 324 100. E-mail: amanpuri@amanresorts.com

PAVILIONS THAT PUT YOU IN TOUCH WITH NATURE

When Adrian Zecha acquired the beautiful palm grove on Pansea Beach, he gave Ed Tuttle a free hand to build a most private hotel. The pavilions, scattered over the hillside, have terraced extensions and open air living rooms built on cement pillars the color of coconut palm trunks. Each one has a slate-colored, terra cotta tiled roof and the interiors are in maka wood. From the moment you set foot in this timeless place, everything happens like in a fairy tale.

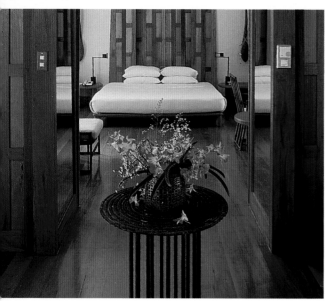

HELPFUL INFORMATION

- Open year round
- 20 minutes from Phuket Airport
- 40 private pavilions: $450–$1,400
- 30 Thai homes: $1,240–$6,950
- 2 restaurants: Thai and Italian
- Swimming pool
- Sauna
- Gym
- Dogs not allowed

PENINSULA BANGKOK Thailand

BANGKOK 333, Charoennakorn Road, Klongsan, 10600. Tel: 011 66 2861 2888. Fax: 011 66 2861 1112. E-mail: pbk@peninsula.com

A SUBTLE MIX OF EXOTICISM AND MODERN CONVENIENCES

This huge hotel, not shy of modern conveniences, stands on the bank of the Chayo Phraya River, where a shuttle offers easy access to the downtown area. The decoration of bedrooms and suites alike is discreet and refined: teak furniture combines with silk curtains and bedding. Here, American architects have mixed New York and Thai styles, as pure, straight lines combine with pagoda-like pavilions. Meals can be taken in five different places. The restaurant offers Cantonese cuisine in a very pleasant setting amid thick vegetation, but the most fun is probably to be had in the lobby, with its small tables and sofas. From this location, you can people watch, unnoticed. When they designed the swimming pool,

HELPFUL INFORMATION

- Open year round
- 370 rooms: $150–$260
- 60 suites: $225–$400
- 4 restaurants

- Swimming pool
- Sauna
- Gym & fitness center
- Dogs not allowed

the architects really showed their imaginativeness and good taste. It is built on three levels, with the last one merging with the river. The pool serves as a link between the civilized world and the untamed nature that is still very much in evidence on banks of the Chayo Phraya.

BEGAWAN GIRI ESTATE Indonesia

BALI P. O. Box 54, Ubud, 80571. Tel: 011 62 361 978 888. Fax: 011 62 361 978 889. E-mail: reservations@begawan.com

CLOSE TO NATURE

In a 20-acre patch of jungle on the island of Bali, the Begawan Giri is one of the loveliest spots in the world. On this "sage's mountain" (*begawan giri*, in Balinese), architect Cheong Yew Kuan has built five villas in perfect harmony with the five elements: wind, earth, water, fire and wood. Each villa is actually made up of five houses scattered in the jungle. Building the complex proved to be a lengthy and arduous task, requiring infinite patience and intelligence to transport stones for the pool from neighboring Java and the six-ton tubs from the Ening villa. For the interior decoration, furniture best suited to each villa was sought out from island to island: old Chinese furniture for Bayugita ("the song of the

wind"), old mahogany and precious seats for Umabona ("house of the earth"), pieces made of massive, rough teak discovered on the island of Suba for Tejasuara ("the noise of fire"). The hotel has been designed to become one with the outstanding natural setting offered by the Indonesian jungle.

HELPFUL INFORMATION

- Open year round
- 75 minutes from Denpasar Airport
- 22 suites: $445 (low season), $495 (high season)
- 5 residences with private swimming pools: $3,960–$4,400
- 2 restaurants
- Swimming pool & gym

BALI AT SAYAN Indonesia

BALI Four Seasons, Sayan, Ubud, Gianyar, 80571. Tel: 011 62 361 977 577. Fax: 011 62 361 977 588. Website: www.fourseasons.com

A PARADISE AMID PADDY FIELDS

The Four Seasons Resort Bali Sayan lies 10 minutes from the town of Ubud. Access is by car, along a narrow road, or on foot, across an amazing wooden bridge that straddles an arm of the river. Water here is so omnipresent that it has become one of the materials of the architecture. The roof is in the form of an elliptical pond scattered with lotus flowers, and waterfalls tumble down the façade to irrigate the paddy fields. This hotel is a little paradise, offering 46 rooms, in the form of suites and villas, built with local materials, decorated with hand-crafted furniture made on the island and hung with drapes made and dyed on the spot. All the bathrooms are made of teak and black marble. The large windows are fitted with slatted wooden blinds and the four-poster beds are draped with tulle, which, at night, serves as mosquito netting.

HELPFUL INFORMATION
- Open year round
- 40 minutes from Ngurah Rai International Airport
- 18 suites: $450
- 33 villas: $575
- Restaurant
- Swimming pool & sauna
- Dogs not allowed

AMANDARI Indonesia

BALI Kedewatan, Ubud, 80571. Tel: 011 62 361 975 333. Fax: 011 62 361 975 335. E-mail: amandari@amanresorts.com

A SUCCESSFUL MARRIAGE BETWEEN ARCHITECTURE AND NATURE

Devised by architect Peter Mueller, this hotel stands in the midst of gardens designed by Made Wijaya. An outstanding harmony emanates from its bungalow suites, which are arranged like a Balinese village and survey the valley and its paddy fields. Designed to make the very most of nature, each house is a happy compromise between Balinese tradition and Japanese minimalism. The materials used come largely from the island: teak, coconut palm, bamboo, volcanic stone, and Java marble. The furniture, designed by Neville Marsh, is sober, comfortable and contemporary. The paneled bathrooms overlook an outdoor pool. The wood, fans, immense interplay of timberwork, and colonial-style furnishings make the rooms friendly and welcoming. Lastly, like a mirror hanging in the air, the swimming pool blends with the landscape of the paddy fields surrounding it.

HELPFUL INFORMATION

- Open year round
- 45 minutes from Denpasar Airport
- 30 suites and private villas: $600–$2,950
- Restaurant
- Swimming pool
- Fitness center
- Spa
- Sauna
- Dogs not allowed

AMANUSA Indonesia

BALI Nusa Dua, 80363. Tel: 011 62 361 772 333. Fax: 011 62 361 772 335. E-mail: amanusa@amanresorts.com

EXOTICISM AND A VERDANT GOLF COURSE AT THE SEA'S EDGE

This fertile Indonesian island, with its equatorial climate, has often been praised by guests. The Amanusa was opened in Bali in September 1992. It is built on a golf course that is situated on a lush hillside a few miles from the airport. It consists of private suites with gardens and views over the golf course, the Nusa Dua peninsula, and the Indian Ocean. We should add that eight of the suites have their own pools. The interior decoration blends exoticism and classic design. Thai and continental meals are taken on a picturesque terrace overlooking the golf course, which is quite magnificent itself. And guests can partake in other sports such as tennis, swimming and cycling. There is also a relaxing bar, a sumptuous pool, spacious and elegantly decorated rooms, culture in the library and treatments of your choice in the beauty center. You can easily spend several idyllic days in this haven of luxury and refinement.

HELPFUL INFORMATION
- Open year round
- 20 minutes from Denpasar Airport
- 35 suites: $600–$1,200
- 2 restaurants
- Swimming pool
- Private beach
- Beach club
- Tennis & cycling
- Dogs not allowed

AMANJIWO Indonesia

JAVA Borobudur, 56553. Tel: 011 62 293 788 333. Fax: 011 62 293 788 355. E-mail: amanjiwo@amanresorts.com

A HOTEL NESTLED BETWEEN THREE VOLCANOES AND A 9TH CENTURY BUDDHIST TEMPLE

In the heart of the island of Java, amid paddy fields, the Amanjiwo looks out onto three volcanoes guarding the temple of Borubudur—a masterpiece of Buddhist art, built in the 9th century. Adrian Zecha, founder of the Amanresorts chain called on Ed Tuttle who, imbued with this architecture, was able to copy it without a hint of plagiarism. He has designed a hotel of sandstone and cement, made up of suites each surmounted by a bell-shaped roof, all distributed over two floors in a circular arc. A huge rotunda, topped by a stupa, surveys the whole complex and houses reception, dining room and bar areas. Each of the pavilions consists of a bedroom separated from the dressing room and bathroom by a sliding screen. Outside, a sand-colored, stone pool beckons guests to take a dip.

HELPFUL INFORMATION

- Open year round
- 55 minutes from Yogyakarta Airport
- 36 suites: $600–$2,450
- Restaurant
- Swimming pool
- Dogs not allowed

AMANWANA Indonesia

MOYO ISLAND Sumbawa Besar. Tel: 011 62 371 22233. Fax: 011 62 371 22288. E-mail: amanwana@amanresorts.com

HELPFUL INFORMATION

- Open year round
- 60 minutes by boat from Sumbawa Besar Airport, Brang Biji
- 20 tents: jungle view: $675–$750 ocean view: $800–$875

- Restaurant (full-board)
- Diving
- Boating
- Windsurfing
- Fishing

- Trekking
- Spa
- Massages
- Dogs welcome

LUXURIOUS TENTS IN THE 19TH CENTURY SPIRIT

Located on a small island off the coast of Sumbawa, the Amanwana is made up of several extremely luxurious and sophisticated tents designed from natural materials like teak and canvas, in the craftsman-like spirit of the country. It is hard to find a television or a telephone here, and guests tend to visit for the atmosphere and style of 19th century lodges dear to the British Empire. It took three years for Belgian architect Jean-Michel Gathy to build this hotel. To do so, he chose the most protected corner of the island, which is, moreover, exposed due south. It should be emphasized that this is also here where you can find the best places for diving, windsurfing and hobbie cat sailing.

BANYAN TREE BINTAN Indonesia

BINTAN ISLAND Tanjong Said. Tel: 011 62 770 693 100. Fax: 011 62 770 693 200. E-mail: bintan@banyantree.com

MUCH REFINEMENT OFF THE COAST OF SINGAPORE

This hotel offers a chance to sample the Asian art of living. The use of natural materials such as lava stone, granite and teak, lends the place its authenticity. The decoration shows a deep respect for nature, with lounge-patios overlooking the sea.

HELPFUL INFORMATION

- Open year round
- 45 minutes by boat from Singapore Airport
- 72 villas:
$370–$820 (with jacuzzi),
$670–$1,575 (with swimming pool)
- 2 restaurants
- Sauna & spa
- Tennis & golf
- Dogs not allowed

THE OBEROÏ LOMBOK Indonesia

LOMBOK Medana Beach, Tanjung, P.O. Box 1096, Mataram, 83001. Tel: 011 62 370 638 444. Fax: 011 62 370 632 496. E-mail: reservation@theoberoi-lombok.com

YOU ARE INVITED TO DAYDREAM AND RELAX IN A HEAVENLY PLACE

It is a real shock when you arrive at the Oberoi Hotel to discover the series of black pools lined with palms, against a backdrop of indigo sea. The pavilions around the pools are all the incentive you need to relax, and the small islands you can see in the distance are an invitation to daydream. The beauty of the tropical garden and the vague sound of rakes and clippers mingling, in the morning, with the exotically pleasing birdsong of the island are a treat found nowhere else. Situated on Medana Beach, in the northwest of Lombok Island, this complex of cottages and villas was designed by architect Peter Mueller. The rooms are all on the same level, built in local stone with thatched roofs and views over the gardens and the sea. They boast modern

comforts and outstanding decoration. The black marble bathrooms, against a backdrop of greenery, are fitted with a small, tub-like pool. Beautiful rattan furniture combines with teak wood for doors, wardrobes, parquet floors and canopy beds, which are bedecked in white tulle and Indonesian fabrics. Just a 20-minute flight from Bali, the Lombok Oberoi offers a very rare quality of holiday, with immense white, sandy beaches, peerless sea and coral gardens. This is a magical place, forgotten by time, ideal for a few days of rest.

THE DATAÏ Malaysia

LANGKAWI Jalan Teluk Dataï, 07000. Tel: 011 604 959 2500. Fax: 011 604 959 2600. E-mail: datai@gmhhotels.com

GREAT COMFORT AND SPORTS IN THE THICK OF THE TROPICAL FOREST

Built in the middle of a tropical forest, the Dataï hotel is a veritable gem, made up of a hundred or so rooms, including 40 villas scattered among the trees. The indoor architecture was designed by Didier Lefort and Luc Vaichère, who devised the furniture and lights as well as all the wooden structures made of balau—teak's first cousin. You can swim in two pools, go trekking in the jungle, cycle in the mountains, or play golf close by.

HELPFUL INFORMATION
- Open year round
- 30 minutes from Langkawi Airport
- 54 rooms:
$400 (low season),
$510 (high season)
- 18 suites:
$629–$1,844 (low season),
$841–$2,278 (high season)
- 40 private villas:
$1,080–$4,800 (low season),
$1,400–$6,000 (high season)
- 3 restaurants
- 2 swimming pools
- Sauna & spa
- Trekking
- Tennis
- Golf
- Windsurfing
- Boating
- Dogs not allowed

HÔTEL DE HIEI Japan

KYOTO Hieizan Ippon Sugi, Sakyo-Ku. Tel: 011 81 75 701 02 01. Fax: 011 81 75 701 02 07.

HELPFUL INFORMATION

- Open year round
- 60 minutes from Kyoto train station
- 26 rooms: $202–$235
- 3 suites: $378–$546
- Restaurant
- Dogs not allowed

FRANCE'S SECOND EMBASSY

To celebrate the Year of France in Japan, Jean-Marc Piston and Yukiko Delmas had the bright idea of building an authentically French hotel. The result is a place where the rooms conjure up the charm of provincial France and gardens were designed with a mix of rigor and harmony by landscape gardener Guillaume Pellerin. Located on Mount Hiei, at the apex of mythical Japan, the hotel makes the most of a magical site above Kyoto and Lake Biwa. In this former place of worship, everything is ideal for meditation. Thanks to architects Christian Duval and Roland de Leu, the building has been designed with a keen eye on transparency and light. This hotel is nothing less than a showcase of France's art of living—in a way, it is an alternative French embassy in the Land of the Rising Sun.

PARK HYATT TOKYO Japan

TOKYO 3-7-1-2 Nishi-Shinjuku. Shinjuku-ku, 163-1055. Tel: 011 81 3 5322 1234. Fax: 011 81 3 5322 1288. E-mail: mail@parkhyatttokyo.com

WHEN THE ZEN SPIRIT FILLS A LUXURY HOTEL

The Park Hyatt Tokyo has been designed as a haven of peace for weary travelers and businessmen. It takes up 14 floors of the elegant "Shinjugu Park" tower in the heart of the city, and offers a sweeping view of Mount Fuji. Kenki Tange, father of modern Japanese architecture, designed this 770-foot-tall complex, which is split up into three glass pyramids housing a bamboo garden, a swimming pool and a New York type restaurant. John Muford designed the interior in granite, steel and glass. The hand-crafted furniture and the artwork throughout the hotel lend originality and refinement. A huge library— with more than 2,000 books about art, history and wines—is at the disposal of guests. But the most surprising feature of this hotel is undeniably its collection of black and white portraits taken in cafés throughout Europe by Véra Mercer. These photos line the walls of the "Girondole" restaurant. Once again, the Hyatt chain shows that it is at the forefront of architecture, thanks to its ongoing desire to summon the greatest talents. This place distinctly shows what the spirit of zen can contribute to the hotel industry.

HELPFUL INFORMATION
- Open year round
- Less than 2 hours from Tokyo Narita Airport
- 12 minutes from Shinjuku train station
- 178 rooms: $428–$521
- 23 suites: starting at $832
- 3 restaurants
- Swimming pool
- Sauna
- Gym
- Dogs not allowed

ASABA Japan

SHIZUOKA-KEN 3450-1 Shuzenji-Machi, 410-2416. Tel: 011 81 558 72 70 00. Fax: 011 81 558 72 70 77. E-mail: asaba@relaischateaux.com

THE ORIENTAL ART OF LIVING

There has been much talk in the West about the Japanese art of living, but few have really sampled it. The Asaba Hotel, located in the Izu region, near Tokyo offers a treatment for relaxation. The owner's great grandfather built this inn at the beginning of the 20th century, and it is his passion for dance that prompted him to create a theater. Airi has endowed the 24 original rooms with a better design and vital modern comfort. Hot water springs supply the bathrooms and make it possible to treat rheumatism and stress in the institute. Floors are made of tatami straw and elmwood parquet. Partitions and lights made of parchment encourage plays of light. All the rooms overlook a small pond. When you enter the hotel, you take off your shoes, put on a kimono, and take a bath. The *nakaï* (servants) then bring you a delicious meal. Later on, they will prepare your futon and a comforter laid directly on the tatami. The owners, avid lovers of contemporary art, have added armchairs by Bertoïa and tables by Charles Eames and Le Corbusier, as well as works by Buren, who has already made two visits to Asaba.

HELPFUL INFORMATION
- Open year round
- 2 hours from Tokyo Haneda Airport
- 10 minutes from Shuzenji train station
- 15 rooms: $615–$800
- 4 suites: $895–$1,025
- Dogs not allowed

JACKSON HOLE 1535 North East Butte Road, WY 83001. Tel: 307 734 7333. Fax: 307 734 7332. E-mail: amangani@amanresorts.com

IMPRESSIVE COMFORT IN A HIGH MOUNTAIN RESERVE

At an altitude of 7,200 feet, and in the midst of a 1,000-acre reserve with deer, elk, bison and wolves, the Amangani surveys the prairies of Jackson Hole Valley. Designed by architect Ed Tuttle—who used Oklahoma sandstone, Pacific conifer and sequoia timber—the building is set into the mountain and does not disrupt the landscape. With its slightly sloping roof, covered with cedar shingles, the hotel looks a bit like a Tibetan monastery. Guests at this stunning retreat can light a fire in the hearth and throw open the windows to listen to the snow falling by night. For those with a love for nature, in all its glorious beauty there may not be a more splendid sound.

HELPFUL INFORMATION

- Open year round
- 20 minutes from Jackson Hole Airport
- 40 suites: $700–$1,100
- Restaurant
- Swimming pool
- Spa
- Gym
- Dogs not allowed

AN IDEAL PLACE FOR ANYONE WITH A REAL TRAPPER'S SPIRIT

In northern New York State, and in the snows of the Adirondacks, the former retreat of the Rockefeller family—built with log and stone in 1933, has today become a hotel where you can make the most of the tranquility of Lake Saranac. There are 11 wonderfully decorated bedrooms in four buildings. In the winter, there is skiing, ice skating and fishing. In the summer, you can swim, walk, play golf and tennis, and go horseback riding. There's no television or phone here, and no newspapers, either. But books everywhere, log fires blaze in every room and succulent dishes are concocted by the Albert Roux team. This is truly a remarkable and timeless hotel offering an unconventional and slightly out-of-kilter form of luxury.

HELPFUL INFORMATION
- Open from 4/15 to 3/15
- 3 hours from Albany Airport
- 15 minutes from Adirondacks Regional Airport
- 11 rooms: $1,200–$2,300
- Restaurant (full board)
- Fishing
- Waterskiing
- Trekking
- Biking
- Dogs welcome

LAKE PLACID LODGE United States

LAKE PLACID P.O. Box 550, Whiteface Inn Road, NY 12946. Tel: 518 523 2700. Fax: 518 523 1124. E-mail: lakeplacid@relaischateaux.com

FAITHFUL TO THE PUREST ADIRONDACK TRADITION

This small hotel was built in 1882 on the shores of Lake Placid, in the northern New York State. It is furnished in the Adirondack tradition with fabrics and art objects made by local craftsmen. In the autumn, salmon fishing is the thing to do; in winter, you skate and ski; while in the summer months, you can play golf and tennis, and go biking or canoeing. These days, places like this one that so happily combine a love of wild nature with a hospitable setting, are rare indeed.

HELPFUL INFORMATION

- Open year round
- 45 minutes from Saranac Lake airport
- 10 rooms: $325–$400
- 24 suites: $500–$800
- Restaurant
- Sauna
- Skiing, golf, tennis, biking, canoeing
- Dogs welcome (with additional charge)

MARTHA'S VINEYARD 27, South Summer Street, Edgartown, MA 02539. Tel: 508 627 4151. Fax: 508 627 4652. E-mail: charlotte@relaischateaux.com

collector, he would come on vacation to this Massachussetts island, and in 1970 he purchased these five old captains' houses built between 1705 and 1860. It is not unusual to bump into members of the American jet set nearby.

HELPFUL INFORMATION
- Open year round
- 15 minutes from Martha's Vineyard Airport
- 23 rooms: $250–$525
- 2 suites: $450–$850
- Restaurant
- Boating
- Biking
- Dogs not allowed

A RESIDENCE WORTHY OF AN AMERICAN FILM SET

With its huge trees, white painted wooden houses, and great clumps of rhododendrons, South Summer Street is worthy of an American film set. Here, for almost 30 years, the master of the house, Gery Conover, has made an art of old-fashioned comfort. As an antique

NEW YORK CITY 56 Irving Place, NY 10003. Tel: 212 533 4600. Fax: 212 533 4611. E-mail: inn@innatirving.com

A TIME MACHINE

Just two minutes from Gramercy Park and not far from Park Avenue South, with stone and glass buildings soaring skywards around it, you do not expect to find two brownstones, built around 1930, which evoke the world of Edith Wharton's novels. The bedrooms and suites are furnished as in the Victorian period: thick carpets, brass beds, and old books on mantelpieces. If you arrive at tea time, you will discover in the small groundfloor lounge known as "Lady Mendl's Tea Room," regular customers and elderly ladies sampling scones and muffins served on fine china plates. The "Madame Olenska" suite, with its bow window and the "Washington Irving" suite, with its view over the small garden in the rear, will offer you

sweet moments of peace and quiet—a luxurious and hushed pause in this delightful hotel belonging to the Small Luxury Hotels chain.

HELPFUL INFORMATION

- Open year round
- 20 minutes from La Guardia Airport
- 40 minutes from JFK and Newark airports
- 12 rooms and suites: $325–$495
- 4 restaurants
- Gym
- Dogs not allowed

SOHO GRAND HOTEL United States

NEW YORK CITY 310 West Broadway, NY 10013. Tel: 212 965 3000. Fax: 212 965 3200. E-mail: reservations@sohogrand.com

A HOTEL INSPIRED DIRECTLY BY THE INDUSTRIAL STYLE

In SoHo, what used to be New York's factory district in the 19th century, the SoHo Grand Hotel is inspired directly by the industrial style. A vast entrance hall supported by carved, red brick columns, a stairwell with extraordinary iron steps embedded with bottle bottoms, spare rooms in gray and beige hues, and black and white photos of famous artists, make this hotel a fine-looking, hip place in a neighborhood that is already all of these things.

HELPFUL INFORMATION

- Open year round
- 45 minutes from JFK Airport and 60 minutes from Newark Airport
- 367 rooms: $374–$529
- 4 suites: $1,399–$1,799
- Restaurant
- Fitness center
- Dogs welcome

NEW YORK CITY 147 Mercer Street, NY 10012. Tel: 212 966 6060. Fax: 212 965 3838. Website: www.mercerhotel.com

ZEN DECORATIONS FOR THIS VERY HIP HOTEL

Located downtown near the art galleries of West Broadway, this trendy hotel sidesteps the ostentatiousness of other New York City's establishments with zen design, thought up by decorator Christian Liaigre. Clean

HELPFUL INFORMATION
- Open year round
- 40 minutes from JFK airport
- 75 rooms: 1 $395–$565
- 5 suites: $1,100–$2,200
- Restaurant
- Dogs welcome

lines and clarity reign here. The bedrooms are spacious and calming. Inventive and delicious cuisine by chef Jean Georges makes it a delight to eat in the hotel's restaurant.

STRAWBERRY HILL HOTEL Jamaica

St Andrew Irish Town. Tel: 876 9448 400. Fax: 876 9448 408. E-mail: strawberryhill@islandoutpost.com

VILLAS IN THE COLONIAL SPIRIT, IN THE MIDST OF PALMS AND BOUGAINVILLAEA

Strawberry Hill is a place worth visiting. And you realize this as soon as you leave the airport, because the roads leading to it become steeper and steeper. Your spectacular arrival gives you glimpses of villas built right into the Blue Mountains, on land covered with coffee plantations. At the foot of the mountains, you see the capital and, in the distance, the sea. This plantation, dating from 1700, was destroyed in 1988 by a hurricane. Its owner, Chris Blackwell, then asked architect Ann Hodges to rebuild it in a 20th century style. To create a contrast with the white painted wooden walls, decorator Tanya Mélich deliberately chose dark mahogany furniture and black and white photos of American

singers. In the midst of luxurious vegetation, these wonderful villas, designed like veritable jewels in the colonial style, are a welcome respite for lovers of nature and dreamers, day and night.

HELPFUL INFORMATION
- Open year round
- 50 minutes from Norman Manley Airport
- 14 rooms: $295
- 4 suites: $510–$595
- Restaurant
- Swimming pool
- Sauna & steam room
- Spa
- Fitness center
- Dogs not allowed

EXPLORA EN ATACAMA Chile

SAN PEDRO Domingo at Enza. Tel: 011 56 2 395 25 33. Fax: 011 56 2 228 46 55. E-mail: hotels@gotolatin.com

NATURE IN ALL HER GLORY

Along with faraway Greenland and the route to the Indies and the Americas, Patagonia is one of the mythical lands which have caused people to dream for centuries. The Explora Hotel is also part of this dream-like world. In the heart of the Atacama desert in Chile, with its mind-boggling beauty, this hotel encourages journeys, and is a place where adventure and a spirit of discovery are not at odds with comfort. Standing in the middle of a 40-acre estate, the hotel becomes the link between people and the mysteries of nature. You will be offered numerous excursions on foot, by mini-bus or by horseback, to go and discover pink flamingoes, the upland plateaus of the Andes, volcanoes, hot water springs and myriad little villages rich in tradition and folklore.

HELPFUL INFORMATION
- Open year round
- 60 minutes from Calama Airport
- 50 rooms: $1,256 (3 nights)
- Restaurant (half-board)
- Swimming pool & sauna
- Gym
- Dogs not allowed

SOFITEL SANTA CLARA Colombia

CARTAGENA DE INDIAS Calle del Torno Barrio San Diego. Tel: 011 57 5 664 6070. Fax: 011 57 5 664 7010. E-mail: santaclara@hotelsantaclara.com

CALM AND REFINEMENT IN AN ANCIENT CLOISTER

It was as the result of a wish uttered by a noble lady of Cartagena that the convent of Santa Clara was built between 1617 and 1621. With its rooms located around a patio surrounded by arches on columns, the cloister is a legacy of Spanish colonial architecture. In 1992 the building was restored and turned into a luxury hotel. Paradoxically, this ancient cloister is now covered in bright colors. Decorated by Miguel Soto, it offers comfortable rooms all with views of the old city, the sea, or the two patios. The restaurant also offers high quality fare.

HELPFUL INFORMATION

- Open year round
- 5 minutes from Rafael Nuñez Airport
- 162 rooms: $340
- 18 suites: $450
- 3 restaurants
- Swimming pool
- Sauna
- Dogs not allowed

MÉRIDIEN BORA BORA Polynesia

BORA BORA BP 190, Vaitape. Tel: 011 689 605 151. Fax: 011 689 60 5 152. E-mail: reservations@lemeridien-tahiti.com

STRAW HUTS FOR LAYING ABOUT ON STILTS

The bungalows of this hotel are scattered along a beautiful, white sandy beach at the foot of Mount Otemanu. The decoration of the straw huts comes straight from Polynesian tradition, with stencilled friezes on the walls, and starfish masquerading as coat racks. Each of the bungalows on stilts has a glass panel in the floor through which you can look down into the sublime depths of the sea.

HELPFUL INFORMATION

- Open year round
- 20 minutes by boat from Bora Bora Airport
- 100 bungalows:
  on the beach: $600
  on stilts: $700
- 2 restaurants (half-board or full board)
- Swimming pool & gym
- Dogs not allowed

HOTEL BORA BORA Polynesia

BORA BORA Point Raiti, BP1, Nunue 98730. Tel: 011 689 604 460. Fax: 011 689 604 466. E-mail: hotelborabora@amanresorts.com

HELPFUL INFORMATION

- Open year round
- 15 minutes by boat from Bora Bora Airport
- 21 villas: $750–$850
- 33 bungalows: $500–$850
- 2 restaurants (half-board and full board)
- Gym
- Dogs not allowed

A PARADISE BENEATH THE PALMS, WITH VIEWS OVER THE CORAL REEF

The Hotel Bora Bora bungalows are spread about in the gardens and along the beach, and some, on stilts, are built over the ocean. Comfortable and refined, they are the work of architect Jean-Michel Gathy. The sea breeze gently ventilates these beautiful, red cedar constructions covered with pandanus leaves. The teak furniture goes perfectly in these pavilions, which are so compatible with the nature surrounding them. In the bedrooms, the tulle veils around the four-poster beds act as mosquito nets. After a few days spent in this divine spot, you will better understand why those 17th and 18th century navigators regarded these exotic islands as paradise regained.

INDEX

EUROPE 8

BELGIUM   **64**
Bruges
  Romantik Pandhotel   66
Stevoort
  Scholteshof   64

ENGLAND   **72**
London
  Blakes   76
  Canary Wharf   73
  Charlotte Street   82
  Covent Garden   78
  Hempel (The)   74
  Knightsbridge Hotel   80
  One Aldwych   77
  Pelham Hotel (The)   72
Lavenham
  Swan   84

FRANCE   **8**
Paris
  Astor Sofitel   17
  Baltimore Sofitel (Le)   21
  Bel-Ami (Le)   12
  Costes (Le)   8
  Dockhan's (Le)   26
  Hôtel (L')   14
  Hôtel Champs-Élysées   24
  Hôtel Thérèse   10
  Hôtel Verneuil   16
  Lancaster (Le)   19

  Lavoisier (Le)   18
  Pavillon de Paris (Le)   20
  Pergolèse (Le)   22
  Sainte-Beuve (Le)   13
  Square (Le)   23

Beaujolais
Bagnols-en-Beaujolais
  Château de Bagnols (Le)   36

Bretagne
Locquirec
  Grand Hôtel des bains (Le)   62
Saint-Meloir-des-Ondes
  Maison Richeux (La)   61

Charentes
Ile de Ré
  Chat Botté (Le)   60

Landes
Bordeaux-Martillac
  Sources de Caudalie (Les)   58
Eugénie-les-Bains
  Couvent des Herbes (Le)   54
  Ferme aux Grives (La)   56

Loire
Roanne
  Troisgros (Les)   34

Luberon
Bonnieux
  Bastide de Capelongue (La)   37

Périgord
Sourzac
  Chaufourg (Le)   51
Trémolat
  Vieux Logis (Le)   52

Provence
Aix-en-Provence
  Villa Gallici (La)   38
Arles
  Grand Hôtel Nord Pinus   50
  Mas de Peint (Le)   48
Avignon
  Mirande (La)   47
Baux-de-Provence (Les)
  Oustau de Baumanière (L')   40
Crillon-le-Brave
  Hostellerie (L')   46
Haut-de-Cagnes-sur-Mer
  Villa Estelle (La)   42
Moustiers-Sainte-Marie
  Bastide de Moustiers (La)   44

Savoie
Megève
  Fermes de Marie (Les)   32
  Lodge Park (Le)   28
  Hôtel Mont-Blanc   30
Méribel
  Chalet (Le)   33

GERMANY   **94**
Berlin
  Hotel Dorint   94

IRELAND	88
Gorey	
Marfield House	88

ITALY	96
Florence	
Gallery Hotel Art	97
Torre di Bellosguardo	96
Gardone Riviera	
Villa Fiordaliso	100
Rome	
Posta Vecchia (La)	98
Venice	
Hotel Cipriani	102

NETHERLANDS	67
Amsterdam	
Blakes	68
Seven One Seven	67
Haarlem	
Spaarne 8	70

NORWAY	89
Balestrand	
Kvikne's Hotel	89
Fjærland	
Hotel Mundal	93
Lom	
Roisheim Hotel	90
Oslo	
Holmenkollen	
Park Hotel Rica	92

PORTUGAL	103
Sintra	
Quinta da Capela	103

SPAIN	104
Seville	
Casa de Carmona	104

SWITZERLAND	95
Geneva	
Hôtel d'Angleterre	95

WALES	86
Llyswen	
Llangoed Hall	86

AFRICA 106

KENYA	114
Nairobi	
Borona	115
Finch Hattons Safari Camp	114
Kiwayu	116

MAURITIUS	120
Belle Mare	
Residence Mauritius (The)	122
Grand Baie	
Royal Palm	120

MOROCCO	106
Essaouira	
Villa Maroc (La)	111
Marrakesh	
Amanjena	108
Jnane Tamsna	106
Maison Arabe (La)	110

SOUTH AFRICA	117
Benmore	
Singita	117

TANZANIA	112
Arusha	
Ngorongoro Crater	
Lodge	112

ZIMBABWE	118
Victoria Falls	
Matetsi Game Lodges	118

INDEX

ASIA 123

BURMA   **131**
Rangoon
  Strand (The)   131

CAMBODIA   **132**
Siem Reap
  Pansea Angkor   132

INDIA   **126**
Agra
  Amarvilas Resort   126
Jaipur
  Rajvilas   130
Udaipur
  Devi Garh   128

INDONESIA   **137**
Bali
  Amandari   140
  Amanusa   141
  Bali at Sayan   138
  Begawan Giri Estate   137
Bintan Island
  Banyan Tree Bintan   145
Java
  Amanjiwo   142
Lombok
  Oberoï Lombok (The)   146
Moyo Island
  Amanwana   144

JAPAN   **149**
Kyoto
  Hôtel de Hiei   149
Shizuoka-ken
  Asaba   152
Tokyo
  Park Hyatt Tokyo   150

MALAYSIA   **148**
Dataï
  Dataï (The)   148

SEYCHELLES   **123**
Frégate Island
  Frégate Island (The)   123
Praslin Island
  Lemuria Resort
  of Praslin   124

THAILAND   **134**
Bangkok
  Peninsula Bangkok   136
Phuket
  Amanpuri   134

AMERICA 154

CHILE   **166**
San Pedro
  Explora en Atacama   166

COLOMBIA   **167**
Cartagena de Indias
  Sofitel Santa Clara   167

JAMAICA   **164**
St Andrew
  Strawberry Hill Hotel   164

UNITED STATES 154
Jackson Hole
  Amangani   154
Lake Placid
  Lake Placid Lodge   158
Martha's Vineyard
  Charlotte Inn (The)   159
New York City
  Inn at Irving Place (The)   160
  Mercer (The)   163
  Soho Grand Hotel   162
Saranac Lake
  Point (The)   156

POLYNESIA 168

Bora Bora
  Hotel Bora Bora   170
  Méridien Bora Bora   168

Photographs by:

Daniel Aron: pp. 150, 151, 152, 153
Alexandre Bailhache: pp. 38, 39, 76, 96
Guy Bouchet: pp. 114, 115, 122
Gilles de Chabaneix: pp. 32, 116, 140, 149
Philippe Costes: pp. 97, 137
Pierre-Olivier Deschamps / Vu: p. 130
Jacques Dirand: pp. 26, 27, 50.
Don Freeman: p. 163
Guillaume de Laubier: pp. 13, 16, 17, 18, 19, 20, 22, 23, 28, 29, 30, 31, 33, 34, 35, 36, 40, 41, 46, 47, 51, 52, 53, 54, 55, 56, 57, 58, 59, 61, 64, 65, 66, 70, 71, 72, 77, 78, 79, 84, 85, 86, 87, 88, 89, 90, 91, 92, 93, 98, 99, 100, 101, 102, 103, 104, 105, 117, 120, 121, 131, 132, 133, 134, 135, 136, 138, 139, 141, 142, 143, 144, 146, 147, 148, 159, 160, 161, 164, 165, 166, 167
Marianne Haas: pp. 8, 9, 42, 43, 44, 45, 48, 49, 67, 68, 69, 74, 75, 95, 108, 109, 110, 111, 154, 155, 156, 157, 158, 162, 168, 169, 170, 171
Éric d'Hérouville: pp. 112, 113, 118, 119, 145
Seline Keller: p. 37
Patrice Pascal: p. 60
Gilles Trillard: pp. 10, 11, 12, 21, 24, 25, 62, 63, 73, 80, 81, 82, 83, 106, 107
Deïdi Von Schaewen: pp. 94, 123, 124, 125, 126, 127, 128, 129

Words by:

Alexandra d'Arnoux: p. 47
François Baudot: p. 163
Marie-Claire Blanckaert: pp. 8, 9, 10, 11, 12, 13, 16, 17, 18, 19, 20, 21, 22, 23, 24, 25, 26, 27, 28, 29, 30, 31, 33, 34, 35, 36, 37, 40, 41, 42, 43, 44, 45, 46, 48, 49, 51, 52, 53, 54, 55, 56, 57, 58, 59, 61, 62, 63, 64, 65, 66, 68, 69, 70, 71, 72, 73, 74, 75, 77, 78, 79, 80, 81, 82, 83, 84, 85, 86, 87, 88, 89, 90, 91, 92, 93, 94, 95, 96, 98, 99, 100, 101, 102, 103, 104, 105, 106, 107, 108, 109, 110, 111, 120, 121, 123, 124, 125, 126, 127, 128, 129, 130, 131, 132, 133, 134, 135, 136, 138, 139, 141, 142, 143, 144, 146, 147, 148, 149, 150, 151, 152, 153, 154, 155, 156, 157, 158, 160, 161, 162, 164, 165, 166, 167, 168, 169, 170, 171
Barbara Bourgois: p. 60
Milu Cachat: p. 67
Catherine de Chabaneix: pp. 32, 116, 140
Frédéric Couderc: pp. 118, 119
Laurence Dougier: pp. 112, 113
Éric d'Hérouville: p. 145
Marie Kalt: pp. 38, 39, 50, 76
Marie-Paule Pellé: pp. 14, 15, 114, 115, 122
Catherine Scotto: pp. 97, 137
Francine Vormèse: pp. 117, 159

Elle Decor (U.S.) and *Elle Décoration* (France) are both imprints of the Hachette Filipacchi group.
The content of this book was taken solely from *Elle Décoration* and appeared only in France.

Under the direction of
Jean Demachy

have collaborated to the French edition of this book:

Editorial direction
Marie-Claire Blanckaert
Art direction
Sylvie Eloy-Ridel
Marie-France Fèvre-Couanault
Editorial
Laurence Basset
Sophie Lilienfeld
Copyediting
Isabelle Lévy
and Albane Marret
Photo research
Geneviève Tartrat
Louis Hini
Text research
Sandrine Hess